MORE

Diabetic Meals *in*

30 *Minutes–Or Less!*

Robyn Webb

American
Diabetes
Association

Book Acquisitions	Robert J. Anthony
Editor	Laurie Guffey
Production Director	Carolyn R. Segree
Production Manager	Peggy M. Rote
Text Design and Composition	Harlowe Typography, Inc.
Cover Design	Wickham & Associates, Inc.
Printer	Transcontinental Printing, Inc.

Printed in Canada

1 3 5 7 9 10 8 6 4 2

The suggestions and information contained in this publication are generally consistent with the *Clinical Practice Recommendations* and other policies of the American Diabetes Association, but they do not represent the policy or position of the Association or any of its boards or committees. Reasonable steps have been taken to ensure the accuracy of the information presented. However, the American Diabetes Association cannot ensure the safety or efficacy of any product or service described in this publication. Individuals are advised to consult a physician or other appropriate health care professional before undertaking any diet or exercise program or taking any medication referred to in this publication. Professionals must use and apply their own professional judgment, experience, and training and should not rely solely on the information contained in this publication before prescribing any diet, exercise, or medication. The American Diabetes Association—its officers, directors, employees, volunteers, and members—assumes no responsibility or liability for personal or other injury, loss, or damage that may result from the suggestions or information in this publication.

ADA titles may be purchased for business or promotional use or for special sales. For information, please write to Lee Romano Sequeira, Special Sales & Promotions, at the address below.

American Diabetes Association
1701 N. Beauregard Street
Alexandria, Virginia 22311

Library of Congress Cataloging-in-Publication Data

Webb, Robyn.
    More diabetic meals in 30 minutes—or less! / Robyn Webb.
        p.   cm.
    Includes index.
    ISBN 1-58040-029-9 (pbk.)
    1. Diabetes—Diet therapy Recipes.   2. Quick and easy cookery.
I. Title.   II. Title: More diabetic meals in thirty minues—or less!
RC662.W356   1999
641.5'6314—dc21
                                                                99-42702
                                                                       CIP

To my readers with diabetes, who are my inspiration.

—RW

Contents

A Note about Food Labels

Many food labels in the grocery store use terms that can be confusing. To help you shop and eat better, here is a list of the common terms as defined by the Food and Drug Administration.

Sugar
Sugar Free: Less than 0.5 grams of sugar per serving.
No Added Sugar, Without Added Sugar, No Sugar Added: This does not mean the same as "sugar free." A label bearing these words means that no sugars were added during processing, or that processing does not increase the sugar content above the amount the ingredients naturally contain. Consult the nutrition information panel to see the total amount of sugar in this product.
Reduced Sugar: At least 25% less sugar per serving than the regular product.

Calories
Calorie Free: Fewer than 5 calories per serving.
Low Calorie: 40 calories or less per serving. (If servings are smaller than 30 grams, or smaller than 2 tablespoons, this means 40 calories or less per 50 grams of food.)
Reduced Calorie, Fewer Calories: At least 25% fewer calories per serving than the regular product.

Fat
Fat Free, Nonfat: Less than 0.5 grams of fat per serving.
Low Fat: 3 grams or less of fat per serving. (If servings are smaller than 30 grams, or smaller than 2 tablespoons, this means 3 grams or less of fat per 50 grams of food.)
Reduced Fat, Less Fat: At least 25% less of fat per serving than the regular product.

Cholesterol
Cholesterol Free: Less than 2 milligrams of cholesterol, and 2 grams or less of saturated fat per serving.
Low Cholesterol: 20 milligrams or less of cholesterol, and 2 grams or less of saturated fat per serving.
Reduced Cholesterol, Less Cholesterol: At least 25% less cholesterol, and 2 grams or less of saturated fat per serving than the regular product.

Sodium

Sodium Free: Less than 5 milligrams of sodium per serving.
Low Sodium: 140 milligrams or less of sodium per serving.
Very Low Sodium: 35 milligrams or less of sodium per serving.
Reduced Sodium, Less Sodium: At least 25% less sodium per serving than the regular product.

Light or Lite Foods

Foods that are labeled "Light" or "Lite" are usually either lower in fat or lower in calories than the regular product. Some products may also be lower in sodium. Check the nutrition information label on the back of the product to make sure.

Meat and Poultry

Lean: Less than 10 grams of fat, 4.5 grams or less of saturated fat, and less than 95 milligrams of cholesterol per serving and per 100 grams.
Extra Lean: Less than 5 grams of fat, less than 2 grams of saturated fat, and less than 95 milligrams of cholesterol per serving and per 100 grams.

Foreword

Some things never change. When I wrote *Diabetic Meals in 30 Minutes—or Less!* several years ago, I wrote it with the intention of helping busy people solve their everyday dinner dilemmas. Well, with 75,000 copies sold and numbers continually climbing, it is evident that readers are busier than ever. So it is with great pride that I present *More Diabetic Meals in 30 Minutes—or Less!* I hope this new collection of recipes will inspire, excite, and—more than anything else—enable you to have nutritious, delicious meals without spending hours preparing them.

As with the first book, you'll find plenty of recipes to tantalize your taste buds. Try Turkey-Dill Meatballs, Great Wall of China Chicken Salad, and South-of-the-Border Soup. With recipes like Chicken Noodle Tetrazzini, Grilled Red Snapper with Vera Cruz Sauce, and Old-Fashioned Barbecued Sirloin, you'll have enough ideas for each day of the week. For dessert, choose from Jeweled Fruit Tart, Vanilla Peach Pudding, or Fresh Apple Crisp. The handy clock indicator on each recipe gives the preparation time. And each recipe's complete nutritional analysis helps you calculate all your calories, carbohydrates, exchanges, and nutrients.

No need to change your busy lifestyle . . . all you need are quick recipes that fit into that lifestyle. It is my hope that you will enjoy *More Diabetic Meals in 30 Minutes—Or Less!* as much as the first book. Remember, it is never too late to change your eating habits and meal plan to improve your health. Use this book to help you achieve your personal goals, and make it a part of your healthy lifestyle.

Now read, eat, and enjoy!

Yours in good health,
Robyn Webb

Acknowledgements

There are many people who continue to support my work and need to be thanked. I appreciate the help of Laurie Guffey, who carefully edited this book and so many of my others. I'm glad you're on my team! Thanks to Robert Anthony for believing that a follow-up book to *Diabetic Meals in 30 Minutes—Or Less!* was wanted and needed. I am grateful to so many staff members of the American Diabetes Association who continue to support and inspire me. Most of all, thanks to my readers. You're the reason I write.

Appetizers

*B*lack Bean Spread

You can try this recipe as a sandwich spread, too.

12 Servings/Serving Size: 2 Tbsp	
Exchanges:	
1/2	Starch
Calories 42	
Calories from Fat . . 2	
Total Fat . . . . 0 g	
Saturated Fat . . . 0 g	
Cholesterol . . . . . 0 mg	
Sodium . . . . . . 107 mg	
Carbohydrate . . . . . 7 g	
Dietary Fiber . . . 2 g	
Sugars . . . . 1 g	
Protein . . . . 3 g	

1 15-oz can black beans, drained and rinsed
   (reserve 1 Tbsp liquid)
3 Tbsp hot salsa
2 scallions, minced
2 garlic cloves, minced
1/2 cup low-fat cottage cheese
1 tsp hot pepper sauce
2 tsp cumin
1 tsp coriander
Fresh ground pepper and salt to taste

Combine all ingredients in a blender and blend until smooth, using bean liquid if necessary to moisten.

Preparation time: 5 minutes

Creamy Chive Dip

Put this dip in a crock or sturdy Tupperware container and pack it in your picnic basket, along with some crunchy vegetables or chewy pita bread wedges.

12 Servings/Serving Size:
2 Tbsp

Exchanges:
Free Food

Calories 22
  Calories from Fat . . . 0
Total Fat . . . . 0 g
  Saturated Fat . . . . 0 g

Cholesterol . . . . . 2 mg
Sodium . . . . . . 84 mg
Carbohydrate . . . . . 3 g
  Dietary Fiber . . . . 0 g
  Sugars . . . . 1 g

Protein . . . . 3 g

8 oz low-fat cottage cheese
1/2 cup nonfat sour cream
4 tsp garlic powder
4 tsp onion powder
3 Tbsp minced fresh chives

Mix all ingredients together by hand until smooth.

Preparation time: 5 minutes

Creamy Herb Yogurt Dip

Choose your favorite herb to flavor this yogurt dip.

12 Servings/Serving Size: 2 Tbsp	
Exchanges: Free Food	
Calories	25
Calories from Fat	7
Total Fat	1 g
Saturated Fat	0 g
Cholesterol	5 mg
Sodium	75 mg
Carbohydrate	3 g
Dietary Fiber	0 g
Sugars	2 g
Protein	2 g

1/2 cup part-skim ricotta cheese
1/2 cup low-fat plain yogurt
2 Tbsp low-fat mayonnaise
3 minced rehydrated sun-dried tomatoes
1 Tbsp minced fresh herbs (try dill, basil, or chives)
1 tsp fresh lemon juice

Place all ingredients in a blender and blend until smooth. Serve with crackers or raw vegetables.

Preparation time: 5 minutes

Crispy Chips

Make your own chips without the fat!

6 Servings/Serving Size: 8 chips	
Exchanges:	
1/2	Starch
Calories 56	
Calories from Fat . . . 6	
Total Fat . . . . 1 g	
Saturated Fat . . . . 0 g	
Cholesterol . . . . . 0 mg	
Sodium . . . . . . 41 mg	
Carbohydrate . . . . 12 g	
Dietary Fiber . . . . . 1 g	
Sugars . . . . 0 g	
Protein . . . . 1 g	

6 corn (blue or yellow) tortillas
Water
Chili powder

1. Preheat the oven to 450 degrees. Dip each tortilla quickly in water (this helps to crisp the chip).
2. Stack the tortillas on top of each other. Cut the stack into 8 triangles. Lay the triangles on a nonstick cookie sheet.
3. Sprinkle the chips with chili powder. Bake in the oven for 5–8 minutes until crisp.

Preparation time: 5 minutes

Marinated Chicken Livers

These easy-to-eat appetizers are lower in fat than the traditional version.

6 Servings/Serving Size: 2 chicken liver halves	
Exchanges:	
1	Medium-Fat Meat
Calories	76
Calories from Fat	34
Total Fat	4 g
Saturated Fat	1 g
Cholesterol	189 mg
Sodium	245 mg
Carbohydrate	1 g
Dietary Fiber	0 g
Sugars	1 g
Protein	9 g

1/2 cup dry sherry
3 Tbsp unsweetened pineapple juice
1 Tbsp minced fresh ginger
2 Tbsp lite soy sauce
6 chicken livers, cut in half
6 slices turkey bacon, cut in half

1. Combine the sherry, juice, ginger, and soy sauce. Add the chicken livers and marinate in the refrigerator for 2 hours. Preheat the oven to 350 degrees. Wrap each chicken liver with a piece of bacon and insert a toothpick through the center to secure it.
2. Place the chicken livers on a nonstick cookie sheet and bake for 10–12 minutes until the bacon is cooked through. Cool slightly before serving.

Preparation time: 15 minutes

Ocean Crab Dip

This dip tastes rich, but is surprisingly low in fat.

6 Servings/Serving Size:
2 Tbsp

Exchanges:
1   Lean Meat

Calories	60
Calories from Fat	18
Total Fat	2 g
Saturated Fat	0 g
Cholesterol	14 mg
Sodium	212 mg
Carbohydrate	4 g
Dietary Fiber	0 g
Sugars	2 g
Protein	6 g

1/2 cup fat-free cream cheese
1/4 cup fat-free mayonnaise
1/2 tsp lemon juice
1/4 tsp Worcestershire sauce
Dash cayenne pepper
1/2 cup lump crabmeat, any shells or
    cartilage removed
3 Tbsp slivered almonds

1. Preheat the oven to 300 degrees. In a
   bowl, beat the cream cheese until light
   and fluffy. Add the mayonnaise, lemon
   juice, Worcestershire sauce, and cayenne
   pepper. Beat until smooth.
2. Fold in the crab and almonds. Place in
   a small casserole dish and bake for
   10 minutes. Serve with crackers or raw
   vegetables.

Preparation time: 10 minutes

Seashore Shrimp Spread

Pack this delicious dip into a crock or sturdy Tupperware container to carry down to the beach!

8 Servings/Serving Size: 1/4 cup	
Exchanges:	
1/2	Starch
1	Very Lean Meat
Calories 71	
Calories from Fat . . . 2	
Total Fat . . . . 0 g	
Saturated Fat . . . . 0 g	
Cholesterol . . . . 18 mg	
Sodium . . . . . . 304 mg	
Carbohydrate . . . . . 8 g	
Dietary Fiber . . . . . 0 g	
Sugars . . . . 4 g	
Protein . . . . 8 g	

1 cup fat-free cream cheese
1 cup low-fat sour cream
2 tsp lemon juice
1/2 cup minced cooked shrimp
2 tsp lemon pepper

Combine all ingredients and mix together until smooth. Serve with raw vegetables or pita bread wedges.

Preparation time: 5 minutes

Southwestern Bruschetta

This is a wonderful way to begin a Southwestern meal.

6 Servings/Serving Size: 2 slices	
Exchanges:	
3	Starch
1	Monounsaturated Fat
Calories	282
Calories from Fat	86
Total Fat	10 g
Saturated Fat	2 g
Cholesterol	1 mg
Sodium	411 mg
Carbohydrate	43 g
Dietary Fiber	3 g
Sugars	5 g
Protein	7 g

1 long loaf crusty French bread, cut into 12 slices
3 Tbsp olive oil
1 1/2 Tbsp fresh lime juice
1 Tbsp minced cilantro
1/2 cup chopped plum tomatoes
1/2 cup frozen corn, thawed
1/2 cup minced green peppers
2 garlic cloves, minced
6–10 drops hot pepper sauce

1. Preheat the oven to 375 degrees. Brush each slice of bread with the oil and toast the bread slices on a cookie sheet in the oven for 5 minutes.
2. Combine the remaining ingredients in a bowl and top each slice of bread with the bruschetta.

Preparation time: 20 minutes

Spinach Poppers

Have your guests snack on these appetizers while the rest of the holiday dinner is cooking. You need mini-muffin tins for this recipe!

6 Servings/Serving Size: 2–3 poppers

Exchanges:
2	Vegetable
1	Medium-Fat Meat

Calories	121
Calories from Fat	52
Total Fat	6 g
Saturated Fat	3 g

Cholesterol	86 mg
Sodium	272 mg
Carbohydrate	8 g
Dietary Fiber	2 g
Sugars	3 g

Protein	10 g

1 15-oz can artichoke hearts, drained and chopped
1 10-oz package frozen chopped spinach, thawed and drained
1 cup part-skim ricotta cheese
2 eggs, beaten
1 garlic clove, minced
1/4 cup minced red onion
1/2 tsp minced fresh oregano
1/4 cup shredded part-skim mozzarella cheese
Fresh ground pepper and salt to taste
Nonstick cooking spray

1. Preheat the oven to 350 degrees. Mix all ingredients together in a large bowl.
2. Spray mini-muffin tins with nonstick cooking spray and fill with popper batter.
3. Bake for 25–30 minutes, remove from the oven, and serve.

Preparation time: 15 minutes

*S*pinach-Stuffed Jumbo Mushrooms

Your guests will love this classic recipe.

6 Servings/Serving Size:
2 mushrooms

Exchanges:
1/2	Starch
1/2 Monounsaturated Fat	

Calories	67
Calories from Fat	29
Total Fat	3 g
Saturated Fat	1 g

Cholesterol	1 mg
Sodium	107 mg
Carbohydrate	8 g
Dietary Fiber	2 g
Sugars	2 g

Protein	3 g

12 jumbo mushrooms, caps cleaned and
    stems removed (reserve stems)
1 Tbsp olive oil
1/2 cup minced onion
2 garlic cloves, minced
1/2 cup frozen chopped spinach, thawed
    and well drained
2 Tbsp Parmesan cheese
1/4 cup dry bread crumbs
1/4 cup diced pimento
1 tsp oregano
Fresh ground pepper and salt to taste

1. Preheat the oven to 350 degrees. Chop
   the mushroom stems. Heat the oil in a
   skillet over medium-high heat.
2. Add the stems, onion, and garlic and
   saute for 5 minutes. Add the spinach and
   saute for 2 minutes. Add the remaining
   ingredients and stir.
3. Stuff each mushroom cap with some of
   the filling. Place all mushrooms in a
   baking dish and bake, uncovered, for
   15 minutes.

Preparation time: 15 minutes

Tomato Crostini

Fresh tomatoes are delicious in the spring and summer.

6 Servings/Serving Size:
2 slices bread

Exchanges:
2 1/2   Starch
1/2 Monounsaturated Fat

Calories 230
  Calories from Fat . . 46
Total Fat . . . . 5 g
  Saturated Fat . . . . 1 g

Cholesterol . . . . . 1 mg
Sodium . . . . . . 438 mg
Carbohydrate . . . . 39 g
  Dietary Fiber . . . . . 2 g
  Sugars . . . . 4 g

Protein . . . . 6 g

12 slices Italian bread (about 1 1/2 inches thick)
2 garlic cloves, cut in half
1 Tbsp olive oil
1 cup finely diced, seeded tomatoes
2 tsp capers
2 tsp minced black olives
2 tsp minced fresh basil
1 tsp minced fresh oregano
Fresh ground pepper and salt to taste

1. Preheat the oven to 350 degrees. Rub each slice of Italian bread with the garlic and brush with some of the olive oil.
2. Place the bread slices on a cookie sheet and toast in the oven for 3–4 minutes.
3. Combine the remaining ingredients in a small bowl. Place a spoonful of the tomato mixture on each bread slice and serve.

Preparation time: 10 minutes

Turkey-Dill Meatballs

These turkey meatballs are reminiscent of Swedish meatballs, but they're lower in fat.

6 Servings/Serving Size: 3–4 oz

Exchanges:
1 1/2	Starch
5	Very Lean Meat

Calories	283
Calories from Fat	28
Total Fat	3 g
Saturated Fat	1 g

Cholesterol	148 mg
Sodium	292 mg
Carbohydrate	24 g
Dietary Fiber	1 g
Sugars	10 g

Protein	36 g

Preparation time: 20 minutes

Meatballs
1 1/2 lb ground turkey (have your butcher grind this for you)
1/2 cup dry bread crumbs
2 eggs, beaten
3/4 cup minced onion
1/4 cup evaporated fat-free milk
1 Tbsp minced fresh dill
1/4 tsp cinnamon
1 tsp cumin
1 tsp Worcestershire sauce
Fresh ground pepper and salt to taste

Sauce
2 tsp paprika
1 cup nonfat sour cream
1 tsp minced garlic
1 cup evaporated skim milk
1/2 cup water
1 Tbsp cornstarch or arrowroot powder
2 Tbsp water

1. Preheat the oven to 350 degrees. Combine all meatball ingredients and shape into 2-inch rounds. Place in a baking dish and bake for 20–25 minutes until cooked through. Combine all sauce ingredients except the cornstarch or arrowroot powder and water in a medium saucepan. Cook over medium heat until smooth, about 5–6 minutes.
2. Mix together the cornstarch or arrowroot powder and the water. Add to the saucepan and cook about 1–2 more minutes until thickened. Remove the meatballs from the dish and serve with the sauce.

etic Meals in 30 Minutes—Or Less!

Warm Mexican Bean Dip

This is a great low-fat alternative to high-fat bean dips.

6 Servings/Serving Size: about 1/4 cup	
Exchanges:	
1	Starch
1	Very Lean Meat
1	Saturated Fat
Calories 158	
Calories from Fat . . 59	
Total Fat . . . . 7 g	
Saturated Fat . . . . 4 g	
Cholesterol . . . . 21 mg	
Sodium. . . . . . 574 mg	
Carbohydrate. . . . 16 g	
Dietary Fiber. . . . . 5 g	
Sugars . . . . 4 g	
Protein . . . . 8 g	

1 15-oz can nonfat refried beans
1 6-oz package low-fat cream cheese
1 4-oz can green chilies
1 14-oz can chopped tomatoes, drained
1/2 tsp onion powder
1/2 tsp garlic powder
1/4 cup shredded low-fat cheddar cheese
1 tsp chili powder

Mix all ingredients together in a saucepan until the cheese melts. Serve with low-fat tortilla chips.

Preparation time: 15 minutes

White Bean Pate

This spread resembles the wonderfully aromatic French boursin cheese, but contains much less fat.

12 Servings/Serving Size: 2 Tbsp	
Exchanges:	
1/2	Starch
Calories	49
Calories from Fat	5
Total Fat	1 g
Saturated Fat	0 g
Cholesterol	0 mg
Sodium	165 mg
Carbohydrate	9 g
Dietary Fiber	2 g
Sugars	1 g
Protein	3 g

1/2 cup minced scallions
3 garlic cloves, minced
1 15-oz can white beans (navy or cannelini)
2 tsp prepared Dijon mustard
1 Tbsp fresh lemon juice
1 tsp olive oil
2 Tbsp minced parsley
1 Tbsp minced basil
1 tsp minced thyme leaves
1 tsp minced dill
1 tsp minced tarragon
1/4 tsp nutmeg
Fresh ground pepper and salt to taste

Combine all ingredients in a blender or food processor. Process until smooth. Serve with crackers or pita bread.

Preparation time: 10 minutes

Soups & Stews

Chicken and Apple Stew

This is a sweet and nutritious chicken stew.

6 Servings/Serving Size: 3–4 oz	
Exchanges:	
2	Fruit
4	Very Lean Meat
1/2	Fat

Calories	286
Calories from Fat	60
Total Fat	7 g
Saturated Fat	1 g
Cholesterol	69 mg
Sodium	180 mg
Carbohydrate	32 g
Dietary Fiber	5 g
Sugars	25 g
Protein	27 g

Preparation time: 25 minutes

1 Tbsp canola oil
1 1/2 lb boneless, skinless chicken breasts, halved
1/2 tsp nutmeg
Fresh ground pepper and salt to taste
1 Tbsp Dijon mustard
2 cups low-fat, low-sodium chicken broth
1/4 cup apple cider vinegar
6 whole cloves
3 medium carrots, peeled and sliced
6 medium apples, peeled and sliced
1 cup shredded cabbage
1 cup unsweetened applesauce

1. Heat the oil in a Dutch oven over medium-high heat. Add the chicken breasts and saute on both sides for a total of 10 minutes. Sprinkle with nutmeg, pepper, and salt. Spread the mustard on the chicken. Add the broth, vinegar, cloves, and carrots and bring to a boil. Cover and simmer for 15 minutes.
2. Add the apples and cook for 5 minutes. Add the cabbage and cook, covered, for 10 more minutes. With a slotted spoon, remove the chicken and vegetables from the broth. Keep warm. Add the applesauce to the liquid and boil for 5 minutes. Pour over the chicken and vegetables and serve.

This adapted recipe is courtesy of the National Broiler Council.

Chicken and Zucchini Stew

Use yellow squash in this recipe if zucchini is unavailable.

6 Servings/Serving Size:
3–4 oz chicken

Exchanges:

1	Vegetable
4	Very Lean Meat

Calories	 169
Calories from Fat	. . 32
Total Fat	. . . . 4 g
Saturated Fat	. . . . 1 g

Cholesterol	. . . . 69 mg
Sodium	. . . . . . 241 mg
Carbohydrate	. . . . . 7 g
Dietary Fiber	. . . . . 2 g
Sugars	. . . . 4 g

Protein	. . . . 27 g

1 18-oz can tomatoes
1 cup low-fat, low-sodium chicken broth
1 small green pepper, coarsely chopped
2 garlic cloves, minced
2 medium zucchini, coarsely chopped
Fresh ground pepper and salt to taste
2 tsp minced fresh basil
1 1/2 lb boneless, skinless chicken breasts,
  cooked and cubed into 2-inch pieces

1. Drain the liquid from the tomatoes into a saucepan. Chop the tomatoes and set aside. Add the broth, green pepper, and garlic to the tomato liquid. Bring to a boil, reduce heat to medium, and cook for 10 minutes.
2. Add reserved tomatoes, zucchini, pepper, salt, and basil. Simmer until zucchini is tender, about 10 minutes. Reduce heat to low and add the chicken. Cook for 5 minutes.

Preparation time: 20 minutes

Chicken Vegetable Soup

Potatoes, peppers, and corn make this a heartier chicken soup than the traditional broth version.

6 Servings/Serving Size: 1 cup	
Exchanges:	
1 1/2	Starch
2	Very Lean Meat
1/2	Monounsaturated Fat
Calories 200	
Calories from Fat . . 48	
Total Fat . . . . 5 g	
Saturated Fat . . . . 1 g	
Cholesterol . . . . 36 mg	
Sodium . . . . . . 146 mg	
Carbohydrate . . . . 22 g	
Dietary Fiber . . . . . 2 g	
Sugars . . . . 8 g	
Protein . . . . 19 g	

2 tsp olive oil
1/2 cup chopped onion
2 Tbsp minced fresh parsley
1 cup cubed, peeled russet potatoes
1 cup chopped red pepper
1/2 lb cooked chicken, cut into 2-inch cubes
1 cup fresh or frozen corn
2 cups low-fat, low-sodium chicken broth
1 1/2 cups evaporated fat-free milk
2 tsp cornstarch or arrowroot powder
4 tsp water

1. Heat the oil in a stockpot over medium-high heat. Add the onion and parsley and saute for 5 minutes. Add the potatoes and saute for 5 more minutes. Add the red pepper and saute for 5 more minutes.
2. Add the remaining ingredients except for the cornstarch or arrowroot powder and water. Bring to a simmer and cook an additional 5–8 minutes. Mix together the cornstarch or arrowroot powder and water until smooth. Add to the soup and cook until thickened.

Preparation time: 15 minutes

Chickpea and Pasta Soup

Fresh rosemary turns this soup into a Tuscan feast!

6 Servings/Serving Size: 1 cup

Exchanges:
1 1/2	Starch
1/2 Monounsaturated Fat	

Calories	144
Calories from Fat	36
Total Fat	4 g
Saturated Fat	1 g
Cholesterol	0 mg
Sodium	303 mg
Carbohydrate	23 g
Dietary Fiber	4 g
Sugars	7 g
Protein	6 g

1 Tbsp olive oil
7 garlic cloves, minced
2 Tbsp minced fresh rosemary
2 cups crushed tomatoes
2 cups low-fat, low-sodium chicken broth
1 cup canned chickpeas (garbanzo beans), drained and rinsed
1 cup cooked elbow macaroni
Fresh ground pepper to taste

1. Heat the oil in a large stockpot over medium-high heat. Add the garlic and saute for 3 minutes. Add the rosemary and saute for 2 more minutes.
2. Add the crushed tomatoes and simmer for 15 minutes. Add the broth and beans and simmer for 10 minutes. Add the elbow macaroni and pepper. Simmer for 5 minutes. Serve.

Preparation time: 15 minutes

Cream of Carrot Soup

This bright, delicious soup is the perfect beginning to any meal.

6 Servings/Serving Size: 1 cup	
Exchanges:	
1	Starch
1/2	Low-Fat Milk

Calories 141	
Calories from Fat . . 27	
Total Fat . . . . 3 g	
Saturated Fat . . . . 1 g	
Cholesterol . . . . . 3 mg	
Sodium . . . . . . 218 mg	
Carbohydrate . . . . 22 g	
Dietary Fiber . . . . . 3 g	
Sugars . . . . 11 g	
Protein . . . . 9 g	

2 Tbsp low-calorie margarine
1/4 cup minced shallots
2 Tbsp unbleached white flour
2 cups evaporated fat-free milk, hot
2 cups pureed cooked carrots
2 cups low-fat, low-sodium chicken broth
2 tsp cinnamon
1 Tbsp chopped fresh parsley

1. Melt the margarine in a stockpot over medium-high heat. Add the shallots and saute for 3 minutes. Sprinkle with flour and cook for 2 minutes.
2. Add the remaining ingredients and simmer on low for 20 minutes. Garnish with chopped parsley to serve.

Preparation time: 15 minutes

Cream of Chicken Soup

There is nothing like homemade cream of chicken soup to warm you up on a cold day.

6 Servings/Serving Size:
1 cup with 2–3 oz chicken

Exchanges:

1	Starch
3	Very Lean Meat
1/2	Fat

Calories	213
Calories from Fat	62
Total Fat	7 g
Saturated Fat	2 g
Cholesterol	41 mg
Sodium	209 mg
Carbohydrate	17 g
Dietary Fiber	1 g
Sugars	10 g
Protein	21 g

1 Tbsp canola oil
1/2 cup minced onion
1/2 cup diced carrots
3 cups low-fat, low-sodium chicken broth
2 Tbsp dry sherry
2 cups evaporated fat-free milk
1 1/2 cups diced cooked white chicken meat
2 Tbsp cornstarch or arrowroot powder
4 Tbsp cold water
3 Tbsp minced fresh parsley
Fresh ground pepper to taste

1. Heat the oil in a large stockpot over medium-high heat. Add the onion and saute for 5 minutes. Add the carrots and saute another 5 minutes.
2. Add in the chicken broth and sherry and bring to a boil. Lower the heat and add the milk. Add the chicken and simmer for 5 minutes.
3. Combine the cornstarch or arrowroot powder with the water. Mix until smooth and add to the pot. Cook the soup until thickened. Sprinkle with parsley and ground pepper and serve.

Preparation time: 20 minutes

Creamy Vegetable Soup

This soup is great served with crusty bread and fresh salad on a cool spring evening.

6 Servings/Serving Size: 1 cup	
Exchanges:	
1	Starch
1	Monounsaturated Fat
Calories 128	
Calories from Fat . . 39	
Total Fat . . . . 4 g	
Saturated Fat . . . . 1 g	
Cholesterol . . . . . 5 mg	
Sodium . . . . . . 275 mg	
Carbohydrate . . . . 15 g	
Dietary Fiber . . . . . 2 g	
Sugars . . . . 9 g	
Protein . . . . 9 g	

1 Tbsp olive oil
3 garlic cloves, minced
1 cup chopped cauliflower
1 cup chopped broccoli
1/2 cup chopped carrot
1/4 cup chopped celery
1/2 cup chopped onion
1 10-oz can low-fat, low-sodium chicken broth
2 Tbsp Dijon mustard
Fresh ground pepper and salt to taste
1 12-oz can evaporated fat-free milk
1 Tbsp minced fresh dill
2 tsp minced fresh parsley
1 Tbsp cornstarch or arrowroot powder
2 Tbsp water
1/4 cup Parmesan cheese

Preparation time: 30 minutes

1. Heat the oil in a stockpot over medium heat. Add the garlic and saute for 30 seconds. Add the next five ingredients and saute for 10 minutes. Add in half the can of broth and bring to a boil. Simmer for 10 minutes. In batches, puree the contents of the stockpot in the blender. Set aside in a separate bowl.

2. In the same stockpot, heat remaining broth with the mustard, pepper, salt, and evaporated milk. Bring to a gentle simmer. Add the pureed vegetables and simmer on low for 5 minutes. Add the herbs and simmer for 2 more minutes. Mix together the cornstarch or arrowroot powder and the water. Add to the soup and cook for 2 minutes until thickened. Serve soup in bowls, garnished with Parmesan cheese.

Elegant Leek Soup

Be sure to thoroughly wash the leeks before using them in this soup. They tend to collect a lot of dirt within their leaves.

6 Servings/Serving Size:
1 cup

Exchanges:
1/2	Starch
1	Fat-Free Milk
1/2	Saturated Fat

Calories	156
Calories from Fat	22
Total Fat	2 g
Saturated Fat	1 g

Cholesterol	7 mg
Sodium	186 mg
Carbohydrate	24 g
Dietary Fiber	2 g
Sugars	10 g

Protein	10 g

1 tsp butter
2 shallots, chopped
1 1/2 cups cleaned, chopped leeks (bottoms only)
1 cup blush wine
2 medium potatoes, peeled and diced
2 cups low-fat, low-sodium chicken broth
1 1/2 cups fat-free milk
1 1/2 cups evaporated fat-free milk
2 Tbsp crumbled blue cheese

1. Melt the butter in a stockpot over medium-high heat. Add the shallots and leeks and cook for 10 minutes. Add the wine, potatoes, and broth, bring to a boil, and cook until potatoes are soft.
2. Add all other ingredients except the cheese and heat through, but do not boil. To serve, top individual bowls of soup with blue cheese.

Preparation time: 25 minutes

Lentil Chili

Bulgur wheat gives texture to this meatless chili.

6 Servings/Serving Size: 1 cup	
Exchanges:	
3	Starch
1/2 Monounsaturated Fat	

Calories	271
Calories from Fat	63
Total Fat	7 g
Saturated Fat	1 g
Cholesterol	0 mg
Sodium	218 mg
Carbohydrate	43 g
Dietary Fiber	16 g
Sugars	7 g
Protein	15 g

2 Tbsp canola oil
1 medium onion, chopped
4 garlic cloves, minced
1 cup dried lentils
1 cup dry bulgur wheat
3 cups low-fat, low-sodium chicken or vegetable broth
2 cups canned tomatoes, drained and coarsely chopped
2 Tbsp chili powder
1 Tbsp cumin

1. Heat the oil in a large stockpot over medium-high heat. Add the onions and garlic and saute for 5 minutes. Add the dry lentils and bulgur wheat and stir.
2. Add all the remaining ingredients and bring to a boil. Simmer for 30 minutes until the lentils are tender.

Preparation time: 15 minutes

Pasta Vegetable Soup

This hearty soup will warm you up on a rainy winter night.

6 Servings/Serving Size: 1 cup

Exchanges:
1   Starch
1/2 Monounsaturated Fat

Calories	87
Calories from Fat	36
Total Fat	4 g
Saturated Fat	1 g
Cholesterol	0 mg
Sodium	136 mg
Carbohydrate	12 g
Dietary Fiber	3 g
Sugars	4 g
Protein	4 g

1 Tbsp olive oil
2 cloves garlic, minced
1/2 cup minced scallions
4 cups low-fat, low-sodium chicken broth
1 cup frozen peas, thawed
1/2 cup diced tomato
1 cup diced carrot
1/2 tsp minced fresh rosemary
1/2 cup cooked wagon wheel pasta (or any other shaped pasta)
Fresh ground pepper and salt to taste

1. Heat the oil in a stockpot over medium-high heat. Add the garlic and scallions and saute for 2 minutes.
2. Add the remaining ingredients except the pasta, pepper, and salt, cover, and simmer for 25 minutes. Add the cooked pasta, pepper, and salt to serve.

Preparation time: 15 minutes

South-of-the-Border Soup

This is a spicy twist on traditional corn soup.

6 Servings/Serving Size: 1 cup

Exchanges:

1	Starch
1/2	Fat-Free Milk
2	Vegetable
1/2	Monounsaturated Fat

Calories	203
Calories from Fat	38
Total Fat	4 g
Saturated Fat	1 g

Cholesterol	8 mg
Sodium	278 mg
Carbohydrate	32 g
Dietary Fiber	3 g
Sugars	13 g

Protein	14 g

Preparation time: 20 minutes

2 tsp olive oil
1 cup diced onion
1 medium red pepper, chopped
2 jalapeno peppers, diced
2 1/2 cups low-fat, low-sodium chicken broth
2 cups evaporated fat-free milk
2 cups corn kernels
1 4-oz can green chilies
2 Tbsp cornstarch or arrowroot powder
4 Tbsp water
1/2 cup sliced scallions
1/2 cup low-fat Cheddar cheese

1. Heat the oil in a stockpot over medium-high heat. Add the onion and red pepper and saute for 5 minutes. Add the jalapeno peppers and saute for 5 more minutes.
2. Add the chicken broth and bring to a boil. Lower the heat and simmer for 15 minutes. Add the milk, corn, and green chilies and simmer for 5–8 more minutes.
3. Mix together the cornstarch or arrowroot powder and water. Add to the soup and cook for about 5 minutes until thickened. Garnish each bowl of soup with scallions and cheese.

Turkey and Wild Rice Soup

This slightly spicy soup will warm you up on a cold winter day!

**6 Servings/Serving Size:
1 cup**

Exchanges:

1	Starch
3	Very Lean Meat
1/2	Fat

Calories	202
Calories from Fat	51
Total Fat	6 g
Saturated Fat	2 g

Cholesterol	49 mg
Sodium	146 mg
Carbohydrate	14 g
Dietary Fiber	2 g
Sugars	3 g

Protein	26 g

4 1/2 cups low-fat, low-sodium chicken
   broth
2 tsp olive oil
1/2 cup sliced red onion
2 medium carrots, diced
1 tsp turmeric
1/2 tsp ground red pepper
3 cups diced cooked turkey (preferably white
   meat)
1 1/2 cups cooked wild rice
Fresh ground pepper to taste

1. In a large stockpot, bring the chicken broth to a simmer. Heat the oil in a small skillet over medium-high heat. Add the onions and carrots and saute for 10 minutes.
2. Add the turmeric and ground red pepper and saute for 2 more minutes. Add the sauteed mixture to the broth. Simmer for 10 minutes.
3. Add the remaining ingredients and simmer for 10 more minutes.

Preparation time: 15 minutes

Main Dish Salads

California Walnut, Turkey, and Rice Salad

This crunchy salad is packed with good-for-you ingredients.

6 Servings/Serving Size: 1 cup	
Exchanges:	
2	Starch
2	Lean Meat
Calories 262	
Calories from Fat . . 52	
Total Fat . . . . 6 g	
Saturated Fat . . . . 1 g	
Cholesterol . . . . 34 mg	
Sodium. . . . . . 205 mg	
Carbohydrate. . . . 33 g	
Dietary Fiber. . . . . 4 g	
Sugars . . . . 6 g	
Protein . . . . 20 g	

Salad
3 cups cooked brown rice
2 cups diced cooked turkey (white meat)
1/2 cup diagonally sliced celery
1/4 cup pineapple chunks, drained
1/4 cup mandarin oranges, drained
1/4 cup water chestnuts, drained and thinly
 sliced
1/4 cup thinly sliced scallions
1/4 cup chopped walnuts
6 cups lettuce leaves (try romaine, spinach,
 Boston, or mache)

Dressing
1/2 cup low-fat lemon yogurt
1/2 cup low-fat mayonnaise
1 tsp grated lemon rind
1/2 tsp curry powder

Preparation time: 15 minutes

1. Combine all salad ingredients except the lettuce leaves in a large bowl. Whisk together the dressing ingredients.
2. Add the dressing to the salad mixture and toss to coat. Cover and refrigerate. To serve, spoon 1 cup of salad over 1 cup of the lettuce leaves.

This adapted recipe is courtesy of the Association for Dressings and Sauces.

Chuck Wagon Tenderloin Salad

Wagon-wheel pasta and barbecued tenderloin bring a taste of the old Southwest to your backyard.

6 Servings/Serving Size: 1/2 cup pasta with 4 oz beef	
Exchanges:	
1 1/2	Starch
2	Vegetable
4	Lean Meat
Calories 386	
Calories from Fat . . 92	
Total Fat . . . . 10 g	
Saturated Fat . . . . 3 g	
Cholesterol . . . 101 mg	
Sodium. . . . . . 476 mg	
Carbohydrate. . . . 33 g	
Dietary Fiber. . . . . 4 g	
Sugars . . . . 11 g	
Protein . . . . 40 g	

3 cups cooked wagon-wheel pasta (or use any other shaped pasta)
1 1/2 lb cold cooked beef, cut into 1 1/2 × 1/2-inch strips (use leftover lean sirloin)
1 small onion, very thinly sliced
1 green pepper, very thinly sliced
1 cup low-sodium barbecue sauce
1/4 cup Dijon mustard
3 cups red leaf lettuce
3 cups green leaf lettuce
2 large tomatoes, sliced

1. Combine the pasta, beef, onion, and green pepper in a salad bowl. Mix the barbecue sauce and Dijon mustard together in a separate bowl; add to the salad.
2. Serve the salad over the mixed greens. Garnish with tomatoes.

Preparation time: 20 minutes

This adapted recipe is courtesy of the Association for Dressings and Sauces.

Citrus Swordfish Salad

This recipe uses leftover portions of delicious grilled swordfish, for those too-hot-to-cook days!

6 Servings/Serving Size: 3–4 oz fish with 2 cups greens

Exchanges:

1	Fruit
4	Very Lean Meat
1/2	Fat

Calories	217
Calories from Fat	54
Total Fat	6 g
Saturated Fat	1 g
Cholesterol	44 mg
Sodium	124 mg
Carbohydrate	16 g
Dietary Fiber	4 g
Sugars	11 g
Protein	25 g

1 recipe Citrus Swordfish with Tropical Salsa (see p. 88), chilled and cut into chunks, salsa chilled
6 cups torn romaine lettuce
4 cups torn fresh spinach leaves
2 cups chopped red and yellow peppers

Toss the swordfish chunks lightly with the salsa. Place the greens and peppers in individual serving bowls. Top with portions of the salsa-tossed fish and serve.

Preparation time: 15 minutes

French Tuna Salad

Give ordinary tuna salad a twist with crunchy green beans.

6 Servings/Serving Size: 1 cup	
Exchanges:	
1/2	Starch
3	Very Lean Meat
Calories 146	
Calories from Fat . . 35	
Total Fat . . . . 4 g	
Saturated Fat . . . . 1 g	
Cholesterol . . . 161 mg	
Sodium. . . . . . 368 mg	
Carbohydrate. . . . . 5 g	
Dietary Fiber. . . . . 2 g	
Sugars . . . . 3 g	
Protein . . . . 21 g	

Romaine lettuce leaves
1 10-oz package frozen French-style green
   beans, thawed and drained
1/2 cup chopped celery
1/2 cup chopped green onion
4 Tbsp fat-free Italian salad dressing
2 7 1/2-oz cans water-packed tuna, drained
4 hard-boiled eggs, sliced

Line individual salad plates with romaine lettuce leaves. Combine all remaining ingredients except the eggs and place on the lettuce leaves. Garnish with egg slices to serve.

Preparation time: 10 minutes

Great Wall of China Chicken Salad

6 Servings/Serving Size:
3–4 oz chicken with
1 cup vegetables

Exchanges:

1/2	Starch
2	Vegetable
5	Very Lean Meat
1/2	Fat

Calories	288
Calories from Fat	73
Total Fat	8 g
Saturated Fat	2 g

Cholesterol	96 mg
Sodium	565 mg
Carbohydrate	14 g
Dietary Fiber	4 g
Sugars	6 g

Protein	40 g

Preparation time: 10 minutes

Salad

1 1/2 lb cooked boneless, skinless chicken breasts, cut into 2-inch strips
1 cup diagonally sliced celery
1/2 cup thinly sliced mushrooms
1 cup diagonally and thinly sliced carrots
1/2 cup thinly sliced red pepper
1 cup lightly steamed broccoli florets
1 cup fresh snow peas, trimmed
1 cup bean sprouts

Dressing

1 cup low-fat, low-sodium chicken broth
2 Tbsp low-calorie peanut butter
4 Tbsp lite soy sauce
3 garlic cloves, finely minced
1 tsp crushed red pepper
2 tsp minced ginger
1 Tbsp cornstarch or arrowroot powder
2 Tbsp water
2 Tbsp toasted sesame seeds
1/2 cup minced scallions

1. Combine all salad ingredients in a large salad bowl. Combine all dressing ingredients except for the cornstarch or arrowroot powder and water in a medium saucepan over medium heat. Bring to a boil, reduce the heat, and simmer for 5 minutes.
2. Combine the cornstarch or arrowroot powder and water. Add to the dressing, bring to a boil, then simmer until thickened, about 3 minutes. Pour the dressing over the salad. Garnish with sesame seeds and scallions and serve.

Raspberry Turkey Salad

Drizzle this salad with Raspberry Poppy Seed Dressing (see recipe, p. 59) for a fresh summer main dish.

6 Servings/Serving Size: 3 oz turkey	
Exchanges:	
2	Vegetable
4	Very Lean Meat
1/2	Fat

Calories	212
Calories from Fat	52
Total Fat	6 g
Saturated Fat	2 g
Cholesterol	79 mg
Sodium	169 mg
Carbohydrate	9 g
Dietary Fiber	3 g
Sugars	5 g
Protein	31 g

4 cups fresh spinach, torn
3 cups romaine lettuce, torn
18 oz cooked, sliced turkey breast
3 oz part-skim mozzarella cheese
1/2 cup sliced raw mushrooms
1 cup sliced celery
1 medium red pepper, julienned
1 small cucumber, peeled and sliced
3/4 cup Raspberry Poppy Seed Dressing

Place the spinach and romaine on a large platter. Combine the remaining ingredients and toss lightly. Pile on top of the greens to serve.

Preparation time: 15 minutes

Sweet and Sour Chicken Salad

Sweet apples add a twist to basic chicken salad.

6 Servings/Serving Size: 3 oz chicken	
Exchanges:	
1	Carbohydrate
3	Lean Meat
1/2 Monounsaturated Fat	

Calories	268
Calories from Fat	114
Total Fat	13 g
Saturated Fat	2 g

Cholesterol	72 mg
Sodium	114 mg
Carbohydrate	11 g
Dietary Fiber	2 g
Sugars	8 g

Protein	27 g

Salad
18 oz boneless, skinless cooked chicken
  breast, cut into 2-inch cubes
1 1/2 cups diagonally sliced celery
1 cup fresh snow peas, trimmed
1/2 cup diced red pepper
1 cup diced, unpeeled Gala apples

Dressing
1/4 cup vinegar
1/4 cup canola oil
2 Tbsp sugar
1 tsp paprika
1 tsp celery seeds
Fresh ground pepper and salt to taste

Combine all salad ingredients. Whisk together the dressing ingredients. Pour the dressing over the salad and serve.

Preparation time: 15 minutes

Turkey and Wild Rice Salad

Use leftover roasted turkey and extra rice from stuffing for this hearty salad.

6 Servings/Serving Size: 1 cup	
Exchanges:	
1	Starch
3	Very Lean Meat
1/2	Monounsaturated Fat
Calories	222
Calories from Fat	63
Total Fat	7 g
Saturated Fat	1 g
Cholesterol	49 mg
Sodium	49 mg
Carbohydrate	16 g
Dietary Fiber	2 g
Sugars	4 g
Protein	24 g

Salad

3 cups diced cooked turkey (preferably white meat)
2 cups leftover cooked wild rice
1/2 cup rehydrated cranberries, drained (to rehydrate dried cranberries, pour boiling water over 1/2 cup cranberries, let sit for 10 minutes, and drain)
1/4 cup diced red onion
1/4 cup diced yellow pepper

Dressing

1/2 cup raspberry vinegar
2 Tbsp olive oil
2 Tbsp minced fresh parsley
1 Tbsp minced scallions
Fresh ground pepper to taste

Combine all salad ingredients. In a blender, combine all dressing ingredients. Pour the dressing over the salad and toss well. Serve at room temperature.

Preparation time: 17 minutes

Wild Rice Seafood Salad

Be sure to rinse wild rice well before cooking it.

6 Servings/Serving Size:
1/2 cup rice with 3 oz seafood

Exchanges:

1 1/2	Starch
1	Vegetable
3	Very Lean Meat

Calories	250
Calories from Fat	27
Total Fat	3 g
Saturated Fat	0 g
Cholesterol	159 mg
Sodium	392 mg
Carbohydrate	27 g
Dietary Fiber	3 g
Sugars	5 g
Protein	29 g

Preparation time: 15 minutes

1 6-oz package wild rice
1/2 lb halibut
1/4 cup low-fat mayonnaise
1/4 cup minced fresh parsley
1 Tbsp red wine vinegar
1 tsp lemon juice
2 Tbsp Dijon mustard
Fresh ground pepper and salt to taste
1 lb cooked medium shrimp, shelled and deveined
3/4 cup diced celery
1/2 cup sliced scallions
6 large romaine lettuce leaves
3 small tomatoes, cut into 12 wedges

1. Preheat the oven to 350 degrees. Cook the wild rice according to package directions. Drain and cool. Place the halibut on a baking sheet and bake for about 5–10 minutes until the fish is opaque. Let it cool slightly and cut the halibut into small pieces.
2. Whisk the mayonnaise, parsley, vinegar, lemon juice, mustard, pepper, and salt together in a small bowl to make the dressing.
3. Combine the cooled rice, halibut, shrimp, celery, and scallions in a salad bowl. Add the dressing to the salad and toss. To serve, place lettuce leaves on individual plates, top with wild rice seafood salad, and garnish with tomatoes.

Side Salads

Apple Coleslaw

Children love this nutritious slaw because of its sweetness.

1 cup shredded red cabbage
1 cup shredded green cabbage
1/2 cup shredded carrot
1/4 cup diced Granny Smith apples
2 Tbsp raisins
2 Tbsp apple cider vinegar
3 Tbsp unsweetened apple juice concentrate
1/2 cup low-fat mayonnaise
Fresh ground pepper and salt to taste

1. In a large salad bowl, combine the first five ingredients. In a small bowl, combine all remaining ingredients for the dressing.
2. Pour the dressing over the slaw and toss well. Cover and refrigerate for 30 minutes before serving.

Preparation time: 20 minutes

*A*sparagus and Roasted Red Pepper Salad

This colorful salad is delicious served for brunch.

6 Servings/Serving Size:
1/2 cup

Exchanges:
1 Vegetable
1 Monounsaturated Fat

Calories 67
  Calories from Fat . . 45
Total Fat . . . . 5 g
  Saturated Fat . . . . 0 g

Cholesterol . . . . . 0 mg
Sodium . . . . . . 102 mg
Carbohydrate . . . . . 5 g
  Dietary Fiber . . . . . 2 g
  Sugars . . . . 3 g

Protein . . . . 2 g

2 cups steamed, sliced, fresh asparagus
1/2 cup diced roasted red pepper
1/2 cup sliced artichoke hearts
2 Tbsp olive oil
3 Tbsp fresh lemon juice
2 Tbsp red wine vinegar
1 tsp minced fresh dill
1 Tbsp minced fresh Italian parsley

Combine the asparagus, red pepper, and artichoke hearts in a salad bowl. Whisk together the remaining ingredients to make the dressing and pour over the salad. Chill and serve cold.

Preparation time: 15 minutes

Basil Rice Salad

Basmati rice and basil team up for a light springtime salad.

6 Servings/Serving Size:
1/2 cup rice with 1/2
cup vegetables

Exchanges:

2	Starch
1	Vegetable
1 1/2	Monounsaturated Fat

Calories	254
Calories from Fat	86
Total Fat	10 g
Saturated Fat	1 g

Cholesterol	0 mg
Sodium	91 mg
Carbohydrate	37 g
Dietary Fiber	4 g
Sugars	6 g

Protein	6 g

3 cups cooked brown or white basmati rice
  (use regular brown or white rice if desired)
1 1/2 cups diced carrots
2 medium tomatoes, diced
1 cup canned kidney beans, drained and
  rinsed
2 scallions, minced
2 Tbsp lemon juice
2 Tbsp red wine vinegar
1/4 cup olive oil
1/4 cup minced fresh basil
2 Tbsp minced fresh Italian parsley
2 tsp sugar
Fresh ground pepper and salt to taste

Combine the rice, carrots, tomatoes, kidney beans, and scallions in a salad bowl. Whisk together the remaining dressing ingredients. Add the dressing to the salad and toss well. Chill for 1–2 hours before serving.

Preparation time: 20 minutes

Broccoli Slaw

Often just tossed away, nutrition-providing broccoli stems are put to good use in this slaw.

6 Servings/Serving Size: 1/2 cup	
Exchanges:	
1	Vegetable
1	Monounsaturated Fat
Calories 59	
Calories from Fat . . 42	
Total Fat . . . . 5 g	
Saturated Fat . . . . 1 g	
Cholesterol . . . . . 0 mg	
Sodium . . . . . . 14 mg	
Carbohydrate . . . . . 5 g	
Dietary Fiber . . . . . 1 g	
Sugars . . . . 3 g	
Protein . . . . 1 g	

1 1/2 cups shredded broccoli stems (peel the broccoli stems until smooth; shred by hand or in a food processor with a shredder or julienne blade)
1 cup shredded carrot
1/2 cup diced red and yellow pepper
1/4 cup balsamic vinegar
2 Tbsp olive oil
1 Tbsp minced fresh basil
1/2 Tbsp minced fresh oregano
1 Tbsp minced scallions
2 Tbsp lemon juice

1. In a large salad bowl, combine the first three ingredients. In a blender, combine all remaining ingredients for the dressing. Blend until smooth.
2. Pour the dressing over the slaw and toss well. Serve immediately, or refrigerate before serving.

Preparation time: 20 minutes

Cool Radiatore with Melon

You'll like the flavor surprise of pasta, melon, and citrus together in this dish.

6 Servings/Serving Size:
1 cup pasta with
1/2 cup fruit

Exchanges:	
2 1/2	Starch
1	Fruit

Calories	257
Calories from Fat . .	24
Total Fat	3 g
Saturated Fat.	0 g
Cholesterol	0 mg
Sodium	14 mg
Carbohydrate. . . .	53 g
Dietary Fiber	3 g
Sugars.	19 g
Protein	7 g

1/2 cup limeade concentrate
2 tsp canola oil
1 tsp chili powder
1 1/2 cups honeydew chunks
1 1/2 cups cantaloupe chunks
1 medium cucumber, peeled, seeded, and cut into 1/2-inch chunks
6 cups cooked radiatore pasta, rinsed under cold water

In a medium bowl, whisk together the limeade concentrate, oil, and chili powder. Add all remaining ingredients, toss well to coat with the dressing, and serve.

Preparation time: 15 minutes

Cucumber Salad

This is a great salad served with chicken.

6 Servings/Serving Size: 1 cup	
Exchanges:	
1	Vegetable
1/2	Saturated Fat
Calories 52	
Calories from Fat . . 23	
Total Fat . . . . 3 g	
Saturated Fat . . . . 2 g	
Cholesterol . . . . . 10 g	
Sodium . . . . . . 39 mg	
Carbohydrate. . . . . 6 g	
Dietary Fiber. . . . . 2 g	
Sugars . . . . 4 g	
Protein . . . . 2 g	

4 cups peeled, seeded, and chopped
   cucumber
1 cup shredded carrot
1 cup minced celery
3/4 cup low-fat sour cream
1 Tbsp minced fresh parsley
2 Tbsp apple cider vinegar
1 tsp minced fresh dill
1 tsp paprika

Combine the cucumber, carrot, and celery. Whisk together the remaining ingredients and add the dressing to the cucumber mixture. Mix well. Refrigerate for 1 hour before serving.

Preparation time: 15 minutes

Indian Potato Salad

Ground coriander and turmeric give this potato salad the richness of fine Indian cuisine.

**6 Servings/Serving Size:
1/2 cup**

Exchanges:
1   Starch
1/2 Monounsaturated Fat

Calories 118
  Calories from Fat . . 31
Total Fat . . . . 3 g
  Saturated Fat . . . . 1 g

Cholesterol . . . . . 5 mg
Sodium . . . . . . 47 mg
Carbohydrate . . . . 18 g
  Dietary Fiber . . . . . 1 g
  Sugars . . . . 7 g

Protein . . . . 5 g

1 lb russet potatoes, peeled and diced
1 Tbsp canola oil
1/2 cup diced onion
2 garlic cloves, minced
1 Tbsp ground coriander
2 tsp ground cumin
1/2 tsp turmeric
1 1/2 cups plain low-fat yogurt, stirred until smooth

1. In a pot of boiling water, cook the peeled and diced potatoes for about 15 minutes until tender. Drain and set aside. Heat the oil in a large skillet over medium-high heat. Add the onions and saute for 3 minutes.
2. Add the garlic and saute for 2 more minutes. Add the coriander, cumin, and turmeric and stir well. Add the cooked potatoes and cook for 2 minutes.
3. Combine the potato mixture with the yogurt. Toss gently. Refrigerate for several hours before serving.

Preparation time: 15 minutes

Italian Leafy Green Salad

Look for unique, delicious grapeseed oil in a gourmet or specialty market. (If you can't find it, use olive oil instead.)

6 Servings/Serving Size: 1 cup

Exchanges:
1	Vegetable
2	Polyunsaturated Fat

Calories	106
Calories from Fat	84
Total Fat	9 g
Saturated Fat	1 g

Cholesterol	0 mg
Sodium	35 mg
Carbohydrate	6 g
Dietary Fiber	2 g
Sugars	3 g

Protein	1 g

2 cups torn romaine lettuce
1 cup torn escarole
1 cup torn radicchio
1 cup torn red leaf lettuce
1/4 cup chopped scallions
1/2 each red and green pepper, sliced into rings
12 cherry tomatoes
1/4 cup grapeseed oil
2 Tbsp minced fresh basil
1/4 cup balsamic vinegar
2 Tbsp lemon juice
Fresh ground pepper and salt to taste

1. Combine the mixed greens, scallions, peppers, and tomatoes in a bowl, making sure the lettuce leaves are dry.
2. Whisk together the remaining dressing ingredients. Pour the dressing over the salad and serve immediately.

Preparation time: 15 minutes

This adapted recipe is courtesy of the National Pork Producers.

Italian Potato Salad

Diced red and yellow peppers add flashes of color to this potato salad.

6 Servings/Serving Size: 1/2 cup	
Exchanges:	
1 1/2	Starch
1	Vegetable
1	Monounsaturated Fat
Calories 175	
Calories from Fat . . 64	
Total Fat . . . . 7 g	
Saturated Fat . . . . 1 g	
Cholesterol . . . . . 0 mg	
Sodium . . . . . . 73 mg	
Carbohydrate . . . . 27 g	
Dietary Fiber . . . . . 3 g	
Sugars . . . . 11 g	
Protein . . . . 3 g	

1 lb red potatoes, unpeeled and diced
1/2 cup diced red and yellow peppers
1/2 cup sliced scallions
1 Tbsp minced fresh basil
2 tsp minced fresh oregano
2 Tbsp minced fresh Italian parsley
2 Tbsp olive oil
1/4 cup red wine vinegar
1 Tbsp dry white wine
2 Tbsp Dijon mustard
1 Tbsp sugar

1. In a pot of boiling water, cook the potatoes for about 15 minutes until tender. Drain. Add the peppers, scallions, basil, oregano, and parsley.
2. In a small bowl, whisk the remaining ingredients together by hand to make the dressing. Pour over the salad and serve immediately, or refrigerate for several hours before serving.

Preparation time: 15 minutes

Jicama Slaw

Jicama is a Mexican potato-like vegetable. Large, brown, and round, this vegetable, when shredded, makes a great slaw. You can find jicama in your supermarket produce section. Just peel off the tough brown skin and slice for salads, or shred by hand or in a food processor for this Southwestern slaw.

6 Servings/Serving Size: 1/2 cup	
Exchanges:	
1	Vegetable
1	Monounsaturated Fat
Calories	63
Calories from Fat	4
Total Fat	5 g
Saturated Fat	1 g
Cholesterol	0 mg
Sodium	5 mg
Carbohydrate	6 g
Dietary Fiber	2 g
Sugars	3 g
Protein	1 g

1 1/2 cups shredded jicama
1/2 cup shredded carrot
1/2 cup shredded zucchini, unpeeled
1/4 cup very thinly sliced red onion
1/3 cup sherry vinegar
2 Tbsp olive oil
1 Tbsp cumin
1 tsp minced jalapeno or serrano peppers
2 garlic cloves, minced

1. In a large salad bowl, combine the first four ingredients. In a blender, combine all remaining ingredients for the dressing. Blend until smooth.
2. Pour the dressing over the slaw and toss well. Serve immediately, or refrigerate before serving.

Preparation time: 20 minutes

Middle Eastern Stuffed Tomatoes

You can serve this dish as a light summer lunch or an evening appetizer.

6 Servings/Serving Size:
2 whole plum tomatoes

Exchanges:

1	Starch
1	Fruit
2	Vegetable
1/2	Monounsaturated Fat

Calories	206
Calories from Fat	37
Total Fat	4 g
Saturated Fat	1 g

Cholesterol	0 mg
Sodium	99 mg
Carbohydrate	41 g
Dietary Fiber	8 g
Sugars	15 g

Protein	7 g

Preparation time: 20 minutes

1 cup dry bulgur wheat
2 cups low-fat, low-sodium chicken broth
2 Tbsp olive oil
1 cup diced red pepper
1/2 cup cooked green peas
1/4 cup minced fresh parsley
1/4 cup minced mint
1/2 cup golden raisins (plump first in 1 cup boiling water; let stand for 10 minutes; drain)
3 Tbsp lemon juice
Fresh ground pepper and salt to taste
12 plum tomatoes, halved and seeded
12 mint sprigs

1. In a heat-proof bowl, add the dry bulgur wheat. Boil the chicken broth and pour over the bulgur wheat. Let stand 30 minutes to 1 hour until all liquid is absorbed. Drain off any excess liquid.
2. Meanwhile, combine remaining ingredients except the tomatoes and mint sprigs in a bowl. Add the bulgur wheat and mix well. Stuff the bulgur wheat mixture into the tomatoes. Garnish each tomato with a mint sprig and serve.

Moroccan Salad

This is a delightful, crunchy version of tabouli salad.

6 Servings/Serving Size: 1/2 cup	
Exchanges:	
2	Starch
1	Vegetable
1/2 Monounsaturated Fat	
Calories 207	
Calories from Fat . . 50	
Total Fat . . . . 6 g	
Saturated Fat . . . . 1 g	
Cholesterol . . . . . 0 mg	
Sodium . . . . . 160 mg	
Carbohydrate . . . . 35 g	
Dietary Fiber . . . . . 7 g	
Sugars . . . . 3 g	
Protein . . . . 6 g	

1 cup dry bulgur wheat
2 cups boiling water
6 scallions, chopped
2 1/2 cups minced fresh parsley
1/2 cup minced mint
2 large tomatoes, diced
1 cup peeled, seeded, diced cucumber
1/4 cup olive oil
1/4 cup fresh lemon juice
2 tsp cumin
2 garlic cloves, minced
2 large rounds whole-wheat pita bread

1. Combine the bulgur wheat with the boiling water in a heat-proof bowl. Let stand 1 hour until the wheat has absorbed the water. Combine the remaining ingredients except the pita bread in a large salad bowl.
2. Cut the pita bread into triangles. Place the triangles on a cookie sheet and bake at 350 degrees until crisp, about 15 minutes. Remove from the oven and add to the salad bowl.
3. Drain any excess water from the wheat. Add to the salad bowl and mix well. Refrigerate for 1–2 hours before serving.

Preparation time: 30 minutes

Pea and Tomato Salad

Whip up this quick salad to accompany chicken or fish.

6 Servings/Serving Size: 1/2 cup	
Exchanges:	
1/2	Starch
1	Monounsaturated Fat
Calories	87
Calories from Fat	44
Total Fat	5 g
Saturated Fat	1 g
Cholesterol	0 mg
Sodium	61 mg
Carbohydrate	9 g
Dietary Fiber	3 g
Sugars	4 g
Protein	3 g

1 1/2 cups cooked peas
2 medium tomatoes, diced
1/2 tsp cumin
2 Tbsp olive oil
3 Tbsp white wine vinegar
1 Tbsp Dijon mustard
Fresh ground pepper and salt to taste

Combine all ingredients and toss well. Serve chilled.

Preparation time: 15 minutes

Quick Ziti and White Bean Salad

You can whip up this salad in no time!

6 Servings/Serving Size: 1 cup	
Exchanges:	
3	Starch
1/2	Fat
Calories 281	
Calories from Fat . . 45	
Total Fat . . . . 5 g	
Saturated Fat . . . . 1 g	
Cholesterol . . . . . 3 mg	
Sodium . . . . . 456 mg	
Carbohydrate . . . . 48 g	
Dietary Fiber . . . . . 4 g	
Sugars . . . . 5 g	
Protein . . . . 11 g	

1 15-oz can white beans (navy or cannellini),
   drained and rinsed
1/4 cup sliced green olives
2 Tbsp chopped fresh basil
2 cloves garlic, minced
2/3 cup low-fat Italian salad dressing
2 Tbsp grated Parmesan cheese
6 cups cooked ziti pasta

Combine all ingredients and serve at room temperature or chilled.

Preparation time: 10 minutes

Raspberry Poppy Seed Dressing

Serve this dressing with a crisp spinach salad.

12 Servings/Serving Size: 2 Tbsp	
Exchanges:	
1/2	Carbohydrate
1/2	Monounsaturated Fat

Calories	47
Calories from Fat	26
Total Fat	3 g
Saturated Fat	0 g

Cholesterol	0 mg
Sodium	9 mg
Carbohydrate	6 g
Dietary Fiber	0 g
Sugars	5 g

Protein	0 g

2 Tbsp sugar
1 1/2 tsp Dijon mustard
1 cup raspberry vinegar
1 garlic clove, minced
1 tsp onion powder
1 1/2 tsp poppy seeds
2 Tbsp canola oil
1 cup water
1 tsp unflavored gelatin

Whisk all ingredients together in a medium bowl and microwave for 2 minutes on high. Chill before serving.

Preparation time: 5 minutes

Shredded Carrot and Raisin Salad

This colorful classic is good for you, too.

6 Servings/Serving Size: 1/2 cup	
Exchanges:	
1/2	Fruit
1	Vegetable
1/2	Saturated Fat
Calories	79
Calories from Fat	16
Total Fat	2 g
Saturated Fat	1 g
Cholesterol	7 mg
Sodium	27 mg
Carbohydrate	15 g
Dietary Fiber	2 g
Sugars	13 g
Protein	1 g

1 1/2 cups shredded, peeled carrot
1 1/2 cups thinly sliced, peeled apples (any variety)
1/4 cup golden raisins
1/2 cup low-fat sour cream
1/3 cup fat-free milk
1 Tbsp fresh lemon juice
1 Tbsp sugar
1/4 tsp cinnamon
1/4 tsp nutmeg
1/8 tsp allspice

Combine the carrots, apples, and raisins. Whisk together the dressing ingredients. Toss the dressing with the salad and chill before serving.

Preparation time: 15 minutes

Spinach and Red Swiss Chard Salad

Red Swiss chard is not only delicious, but also an appealing color change from greens. If you can't find it, use spinach.

6 Servings/Serving Size: 1 cup

Exchanges:
1/2	Carbohydrate
2 1/2	Monounsaturated Fat

Calories	154
Calories from Fat	115
Total Fat	13 g
Saturated Fat	1 g

Cholesterol	0 mg
Sodium	65 mg
Carbohydrate	10 g
Dietary Fiber	2 g
Sugars	7 g

Protein	2 g

3 cups washed and torn spinach leaves
2 1/2 cups washed and torn red Swiss chard
1/2 cup sectioned oranges
1/4 cup toasted walnuts
3 Tbsp canola oil
1/4 cup white wine vinegar
2 Tbsp fresh orange juice
2 Tbsp sugar
1 tsp paprika
1 tsp celery seeds
1 tsp dry mustard
Fresh ground pepper and salt to taste

Combine the spinach, chard, oranges, and walnuts in a large salad bowl. Whisk all remaining ingredients together. Pour the dressing over the salad and serve.

Preparation time: 15 minutes

Tri-Colored Rotini Salad

Using colorful pasta makes this dish a little more festive.

6 Servings/Serving Size: 1/2 cup	
Exchanges:	
1	Starch
Calories 92	
Calories from Fat . . 21	
Total Fat . . . . 2 g	
Saturated Fat . . . . 0 g	
Cholesterol . . . . . 0 mg	
Sodium . . . . . . 162 mg	
Carbohydrate . . . . 16 g	
Dietary Fiber . . . . . 2 g	
Sugars . . . . 3 g	
Protein . . . . 3 g	

Salad
2 cups cooked tri-colored rotini pasta
1/2 cup halved cherry tomatoes
1/4 cup diced red pepper
1 Tbsp sliced black olives
1 15-oz can artichoke hearts, drained and
  halved

Dressing
1/4 cup balsamic vinegar
2 tsp olive oil
1 Tbsp Dijon mustard
2 tsp minced fresh basil
Fresh ground pepper to taste

Combine all salad ingredients in a large bowl. Whisk together the dressing ingredients. Pour the dressing over the salad and toss to coat well. Serve at room temperature.

Preparation time: 15 minutes

Tri-Colored Tortellini and Pea Salad

Try adding fresh crab or shrimp to this colorful pasta salad.

6 Servings/Serving Size: 1 cup	
Exchanges:	
3	Starch
1 1/2	Fat
Calories 320	
Calories from Fat . . 98	
Total Fat . . . . 11 g	
Saturated Fat . . . . 3 g	
Cholesterol . . . . 38 mg	
Sodium . . . . . . 251 mg	
Carbohydrate . . . . 47 g	
Dietary Fiber . . . . . 3 g	
Sugars . . . . 5 g	
Protein . . . . 12 g	

1/2 cup balsamic vinegar
2 Tbsp olive oil
2 tsp minced fresh chives
Fresh ground pepper and salt to taste
6 cups cooked tri-colored tortellini
1 cup diced red pepper
1 cup chopped plum tomatoes
1 cup chopped artichoke hearts, packed in
   water, drained
1/2 cup fresh corn
1/2 cup peas
2 Tbsp minced fresh parsley

Whisk together the first four ingredients to make the dressing. Combine all remaining ingredients in a large salad bowl. Add the dressing, toss well, and chill for several hours before serving.

Preparation time: 15 minutes

Pasta

Asian Turkey Pasta

Warm, peanut-flavored turkey tops chewy soba noodles in this tasty dish. Look for soba noodles (Japanese buckwheat noodles) in the international food section of your grocery store.

6 Servings/Serving Size: 1 cup

Exchanges:

2	Starch
3	Very Lean Meat
1/2	Fat

Calories	287
Calories from Fat	64
Total Fat	7 g
Saturated Fat	2 g
Cholesterol	49 mg
Sodium	474 mg
Carbohydrate	27 g
Dietary Fiber	5 g
Sugars	4 g
Protein	29 g

Preparation time: 20 minutes

1/4 cup reduced-fat peanut butter
2/3 cup low-fat, low-sodium beef broth
1/4 tsp ground red pepper
3 Tbsp lite soy sauce
1 Tbsp dry sherry
1 Tbsp cornstarch or arrowroot powder
2 Tbsp water
3 cups diced cooked turkey (preferably white meat)
1/2 cup thinly sliced carrots
1/4 cup diced red pepper
1/4 cup sliced scallions
5 large romaine lettuce leaves
3 cups cooked soba noodles (keep warm)
1 Tbsp toasted sesame seeds

1. In a large saucepan over medium heat, combine the peanut butter and the broth. Stir until smooth. Add the red peppers, soy sauce, and sherry. Bring to a boil.
2. Lower the heat and simmer for 3 minutes. Combine the cornstarch or arrowroot powder with the water. Add to the sauce. Cook until thickened.
3. Add the cooked turkey, carrots, pepper, and scallions to the sauce. Toss to coat well. Place the romaine lettuce leaves on a platter.
4. Place the warm soba noodles on top of the lettuce. Pile the turkey salad in the center of the noodles. Sprinkle on the sesame seeds and serve.

Baked Rotini with Chickpea Tomato Sauce

Try this tomato sauce over rice, too.

6 Servings/Serving Size: 1 cup	
Exchanges:	
5	Starch
2	Vegetable
1/2	Fat

Calories 493	
Calories from Fat . . 63	
Total Fat . . . . 7 g	
Saturated Fat . . . . 1 g	

Cholesterol . . . . . 0 mg	
Sodium . . . . . . 659 mg	
Carbohydrate . . . . 88 g	
Dietary Fiber . . . . 10 g	
Sugars . . . . 14 g	

Protein . . . . 20 g	

Preparation time: 20 minutes

2 15-oz cans chickpeas (garbanzo beans), drained and rinsed
1 18-oz can crushed tomatoes
1 1/4 cup spicy, low-sodium tomato juice
2 garlic cloves, minced
6 scallions, thinly sliced, green and white parts separated
1 tsp cumin
Fresh ground pepper and salt to taste
1/3 cup nonfat plain yogurt
6 cups cooked rotini pasta, undercooked by 3 minutes
1/2 cup plain, dry bread crumbs
1 Tbsp sesame seeds
1 Tbsp olive oil

1. Preheat the oven to 375 degrees. In a medium saucepan, combine the first seven ingredients (use only the white parts of the scallions). Heat to boiling, then reduce heat and simmer, covered, for 10 minutes. In a small bowl, slowly whisk about 1/4 cup of this mixture into the yogurt. Then add the yogurt to the saucepan and stir.
2. Stir in the cooked pasta and toss to coat. Transfer to a baking dish. Mix the bread crumbs, sesame seeds, oil, and green parts of the scallions in a small bowl until blended. Sprinkle the bread crumb mixture in an even layer over the top of the pasta. Bake until edges are bubbly and bread crumbs are golden brown, about 15 minutes.

Bow-Tie Pasta alle Portofino

Fresh arugula is great in the summer.

6 Servings/Serving Size:
1 cup pasta, 3 oz shrimp

Exchanges:

3	Starch
1	Vegetable
2	Lean Meat

Calories	376
Calories from Fat	75
Total Fat	8 g
Saturated Fat	1 g

Cholesterol	214 mg
Sodium	362 mg
Carbohydrate	49 g
Dietary Fiber	4 g
Sugars	5 g

Protein	27 g

1 1/2 lb medium shelled and deveined shrimp
12 sun-dried tomatoes, rehydrated
8 fresh plum tomatoes, cubed
2 cups torn arugula
2 Tbsp minced fresh parsley
1/2 cup fresh Italian parsley
1/2 cup chopped fresh basil
2 Tbsp olive oil
1/4 cup fresh lemon juice
Fresh ground pepper and salt to taste
6 cups cooked bow-tie pasta

1. Prepare an outside grill with an oiled rack set 6 inches above the heat source. On a gas grill, set the heat to high.
2. Place the shrimp in an oiled vegetable basket. Grill, turning constantly, for about 5 minutes. Remove shrimp from grill.
3. Combine the grilled shrimp with the remaining ingredients. Toss well and serve.

Preparation time: 20 minutes

Chicken Noodle Tetrazzini

This is a wonderfully comforting dish on a chilly night.

6 Servings/Serving Size:
1 cup pasta with 3 oz chicken

Exchanges:	
4	Starch
4	Very Lean Meat
1/2	Fat

Calories	496
Calories from Fat	74
Total Fat	8 g
Saturated Fat	2 g
Cholesterol	125 mg
Sodium	279 mg
Carbohydrate	61 g
Dietary Fiber	6 g
Sugars	13 g
Protein	44 g

Preparation time: 20 minutes

2 Tbsp low-calorie margarine
2 Tbsp unbleached white flour
1 1/2 cups evaporated fat-free milk
1 cup water
1/4 cup low-fat, low-sodium chicken broth
Fresh ground pepper to taste
1/8 tsp cayenne pepper
1 10-oz package frozen peas
1/2 cup nonfat plain yogurt
2 Tbsp Parmesan cheese
2 cups sliced mushrooms
6 cups cooked egg noodles
1 1/2 lb cooked chicken breasts, cut into
   2-inch cubes

1. Preheat the oven to 425 degrees. Melt the margarine in a medium saucepan. Blend in the flour until smooth. Stir in the milk, water, broth, pepper, and cayenne pepper. Cook over medium heat, stirring constantly, until mixture thickens and comes to a boil, about 10 minutes.
2. Stir in the peas, yogurt, and cheese. Mix the sauce with the mushrooms, cooked noodles, and chicken. Pour the mixture into a baking dish and bake for 15 minutes.

Creamy Citrus Pasta

Try this pasta recipe by itself or with grilled seafood.

6 Servings/Serving Size: 1 cup	
Exchanges:	
3	Starch
1/2	Fat-Free Milk
Calories 282	
Calories from Fat . . 38	
Total Fat . . . . 4 g	
Saturated Fat . . . . 2 g	
Cholesterol . . . . 10 mg	
Sodium . . . . . . 182 mg	
Carbohydrate . . . . 47 g	
Dietary Fiber . . . . . 2 g	
Sugars . . . . 8 g	
Protein . . . . 13 g	

1 Tbsp butter
1 1/2 cups evaporated fat-free milk
1 1/2 Tbsp lemon juice
1/2 tsp orange extract
1/2 tsp lemon peel
1/2 tsp orange peel
1/4 cup grated Parmesan cheese
Fresh ground pepper and salt to taste
6 cups cooked penne pasta

1. In a nonstick skillet over medium heat, mix all ingredients except the cheese, pepper, salt, and pasta. Stir constantly until heated through.
2. Add the cheese, pepper, and salt and heat a few more minutes. Add the sauce to the cooked pasta and serve.

Preparation time: 10 minutes

*F*ettucine Verde

Serve this perky dish with a bright orange vegetable, such as carrots.

6 Servings/Serving Size: 1 cup	
Exchanges:	
2 1/2	Starch
1/2 Monounsaturated Fat	

Calories	225
Calories from Fat	50
Total Fat	6 g
Saturated Fat	1 g
Cholesterol	47 mg
Sodium	118 mg
Carbohydrate	35 g
Dietary Fiber	2 g
Sugars	2 g
Protein	9 g

1 1/2 cups fresh spinach leaves
1/2 cup minced fresh parsley
1 Tbsp olive oil
1/2 cup low-fat, low-sodium chicken broth
1/2 cup dry white wine
2 tsp minced garlic
Fresh ground pepper and salt to taste
6 cups cooked fettucine
1/4 cup grated Parmesan cheese

1. Wash the spinach leaves, pat dry, and tear into pieces. Place all ingredients except the pasta and cheese in a skillet.
2. Cook over medium heat until spinach is tender. Toss the spinach mixture with the cooked fettucine. Garnish with cheese to serve.

Preparation time: 25 minutes

*F*usilli with Broccoli, Sun-Dried Tomatoes, and Garlic

The flavors in this dish blend wonderfully.

6 Servings/Serving Size:
1 cup pasta with
1/2 cup vegetables

Exchanges:

3	Starch
1	Vegetable

Calories	263
Calories from Fat . .	35
Total Fat	4 g
Saturated Fat	1 g

Cholesterol	0 mg
Sodium.	213 mg
Carbohydrate. . . .	49 g
Dietary Fiber.	5 g
Sugars	4 g

Protein	10 g

1 Tbsp olive oil
3 garlic cloves, minced
1/4 cup minced red onion
2 cups broccoli florets
1 cup chopped, rehydrated sun-dried
   tomatoes
1/2 cup low-fat, low-sodium chicken broth
6 cups cooked fusilli pasta
1 Tbsp grated Parmesan cheese

1. Heat the oil in a large skillet over medium-high heat. Add the garlic and onion and saute for 5 minutes. Add the broccoli and tomatoes and saute for 5 more minutes.
2. Add the broth, cover, and steam for 3 minutes. Toss the vegetables with the pasta and garnish with cheese to serve.

Preparation time: 20 minutes

Gourmet Mushroom Pasta

Use any variety of wild mushrooms for this recipe, or try a combination of shiitake and regular white mushrooms for a fantastic taste.

6 Servings/Serving Size: 1 cup	
Exchanges:	
3	Starch
1	Vegetable
1/2	Monounsaturated Fat

Calories 282	
Calories from Fat . . 42	
Total Fat . . . . 5 g	
Saturated Fat . . . . 1 g	
Cholesterol . . . . . 3 mg	
Sodium . . . . . . 92 mg	
Carbohydrate . . . . 48 g	
Dietary Fiber . . . . . 4 g	
Sugars . . . . 6 g	
Protein . . . . 11 g	

1 Tbsp olive oil
1/2 cup chopped red onion
3 cups sliced mushrooms, stems removed
2 tsp garlic
1/2 cup evaporated fat-free milk
1/2 cup dry red wine
1/4 cup Parmesan cheese
2 tsp cornstarch or arrowroot powder
4 tsp water
6 cups cooked bow-tie pasta
1/4 cup minced fresh parsley

1. Heat the oil in a medium skillet over medium-high heat. Add the onion and mushrooms and saute for 5 minutes. Add the garlic and saute for 1 more minute.
2. Add the milk and wine and cook over medium heat for 3 minutes. Add the cheese and cook for 1 more minute.
3. Mix together the cornstarch or arrowroot powder and water. Add to the pan and cook until sauce is thickened. Toss the sauce with the pasta and garnish with parsley to serve.

Preparation time: 15 minutes

Ground Chicken Stroganoff

Crunchy water chestnuts add wonderful texture to this old-fashioned favorite.

6 Servings/Serving Size:
1/2 cup noodles with
4 oz chicken

Exchanges:

2	Starch
4	Very Lean Meat
1/2	Fat

Calories	322
Calories from Fat	70
Total Fat	8 g
Saturated Fat	3 g

Cholesterol	108 mg
Sodium	183 mg
Carbohydrate	30 g
Dietary Fiber	2 g
Sugars	6 g

Protein	31 g

Preparation time: 20 minutes

1 1/2 lb ground chicken breast (have your
  butcher grind this for you)
1 medium onion, chopped
1 cup thinly sliced mushrooms
1 4-oz can sliced water chestnuts
Fresh ground pepper and salt to taste
2 Tbsp unbleached white flour
1 cup low-fat, low-sodium chicken broth
1 Tbsp white wine
1 Tbsp Worcestershire sauce
1 Tbsp Dijon mustard
1 cup low-fat sour cream
3 cups cooked wide noodles

1. In a medium skillet over medium-high heat, brown the chicken for about 3–4 minutes. Add the onion and saute for 3 minutes. Add the mushrooms and saute for 4 more minutes. Add the water chestnuts, pepper, and salt.
2. Sprinkle the flour over the mixture. Add the chicken broth. Mix together the wine, Worcestershire sauce, and mustard. Add to the skillet. Reduce heat to low and simmer for 10 minutes. Add the sour cream and heat on low for 1–2 minutes. Serve over cooked noodles.

Low-Fat Macaroni and Cheese

Evaporated skim milk and low-fat cheeses make this a healthier version of an old favorite.

6 Servings/Serving Size: 1 cup	
Exchanges:	
2	Starch
1	Very Lean Meat
Calories	203
Calories from Fat . .	24
Total Fat	3 g
Saturated Fat	1 g
Cholesterol	14 mg
Sodium	331 mg
Carbohydrate	28 g
Dietary Fiber	1 g
Sugars	6 g
Protein	16 g

3/4 cup evaporated fat-free milk
1 cup low-fat cottage cheese
1/2 cup part-skim ricotta cheese
1/2 cup low-fat cheddar cheese
1/2 tsp nutmeg
Fresh ground pepper and salt to taste
1 lb cooked elbow macaroni
1 Tbsp Parmesan cheese
1 Tbsp dry bread crumbs

1. Preheat the oven to 350 degrees. Heat the milk in a saucepan over low heat. Add the cheeses until they melt, stirring constantly.
2. Stir in the nutmeg, pepper, and salt. Remove the cheese sauce from the heat. Add the cooked pasta to the cheese sauce and mix well.
3. Pour the mixture into a 2-quart casserole dish. Sprinkle with Parmesan cheese and bread crumbs. Bake the casserole for 15–20 minutes until bubbly and the top is browned.

Preparation time: 15 minutes

Mediterranean Fettucine with Shrimp

This quick dish tastes like it took hours to prepare!

6 Servings/Serving Size: 2 oz shrimp with 1 cup pasta

Exchanges:	
2 1/2	Starch
2	Very Lean Meat

Calories	279
Calories from Fat	46
Total Fat	5 g
Saturated Fat	2 g
Cholesterol	136 mg
Sodium	267 mg
Carbohydrate	39 g
Dietary Fiber	3 g
Sugars	5 g
Protein	20 g

6 cups cooked fettucine
12 oz peeled and deveined medium shrimp
1 10-oz package frozen chopped spinach, thawed
1 cup plain low-fat yogurt
1/4 cup crumbled feta cheese
2 garlic cloves, minced
1 Tbsp minced dill
Fresh ground pepper to taste

Three minutes before the pasta is finished cooking, add the shrimp and spinach to the pot. Drain completely. Toss with the remaining ingredients and serve.

Preparation time: 15 minutes

Pasta, White Beans, and Tuna

White beans add a little extra fiber and protein to this nutritious salad.

6 Servings/Serving Size: 1 cup pasta with 2 oz tuna and 1/4 cup beans	
Exchanges:	
3 1/2	Starch
1	Vegetable
1/2	Monounsaturated Fat
2	Very Lean Meat
Calories	405
Calories from Fat	65
Total Fat	7 g
Saturated Fat	1 g
Cholesterol	17 mg
Sodium	429 mg
Carbohydrate	58 g
Dietary Fiber	7 g
Sugars	6 g
Protein	28 g

Salad

12 oz canned white meat tuna, drained and flaked
3 cups cooked, sliced, fresh asparagus
1 1/2 cups canned white beans (navy or cannellini), drained and rinsed
8 large black olives, pitted and sliced
1/2 cup diced roasted red pepper
6 cups cooked corkscrew pasta

Dressing

1/3 cup balsamic vinegar
2 Tbsp olive oil
2 tsp lemon juice
1 Tbsp Dijon mustard
2 Tbsp minced red onion
Fresh ground pepper and salt to taste

Combine all ingredients for the salad. Whisk together all dressing ingredients. Pour the dressing over the salad and refrigerate for 1 hour before serving.

Preparation time: 20 minutes

Rosemary Pasta

Rosemary is a prized herb in Italian cooking.

6 Servings/Serving Size: 1 cup	
Exchanges:	
3	Starch
1	Vegetable
1	Very Lean Meat
1/2	Monounsaturated Fat

Calories	325
Calories from Fat	66
Total Fat	7 g
Saturated Fat	2 g
Cholesterol	8 mg
Sodium	461 mg
Carbohydrate	48 g
Dietary Fiber	4 g
Sugars	6 g
Protein	17 g

1 Tbsp olive oil
1 medium zucchini, halved and cut into
    4-inch slices
1 medium yellow squash, halved and cut
    into 4-inch slices
8 medium mushrooms, sliced
1 4-oz can pitted black olives, drained and
    quartered
1 28-oz can plum tomatoes, drained and
    chopped
8 oz low-fat shredded cheddar cheese
1 tsp minced fresh rosemary
6 cups cooked rotini pasta

Preheat the oven to 350 degrees. In a large skillet, saute the zucchini and squash in oil over medium heat for 2 minutes. Place all ingredients in a 9 x 12-inch baking dish and mix well. Bake, uncovered, for 15 minutes.

Preparation time: 20 minutes

Spicy Peanut Pasta

For variety, try adding cooked chicken or shrimp to this wonderfully creamy peanut sauce.

6 Servings/Serving Size:
1 cup

Exchanges:

3 1/2	Starch
1/2	Fat

Calories	299
Calories from Fat	57
Total Fat	6 g
Saturated Fat	1 g
Cholesterol	0 mg
Sodium	319 mg
Carbohydrate	50 g
Dietary Fiber	4 g
Sugars	6 g
Protein	11 g

Preparation time: 10 minutes

1/3 cup lite crunchy peanut butter
1/4 tsp coconut extract
1 1/4 cups low-fat, low-sodium chicken broth
1/2 tsp crushed red pepper
2 garlic cloves, minced
1 tsp grated fresh ginger
2 Tbsp lite soy sauce
1/2 tsp hot pepper sauce
2 tsp sugar
Fresh ground pepper and salt to taste
1 Tbsp cornstarch or arrowroot powder
2 Tbsp water
6 cups fusilli pasta
1/4 cup sliced scallions

1. Combine all ingredients except cornstarch or arrowroot powder, water, pasta, and scallions in a medium saucepan. Cook over medium heat for 10–15 minutes.
2. Combine the cornstarch or arrowroot powder with the water. Mix until smooth. Add to the sauce, and cook for 1 more minute until thickened.
3. Pour the sauce over the pasta and garnish with scallions to serve.

Tarragon Dill Pasta with Shrimp

This colorful dish is a complete meal in itself.

6 Servings/Serving Size: 1 1/2 cups	
Exchanges:	
3	Starch
1	Vegetable
2	Very Lean Meat
1/2 Monounsaturated Fat	
Calories 372	
Calories from Fat . . 62	
Total Fat . . . . 7 g	
Saturated Fat . . . . 1 g	
Cholesterol . . . 161 mg	
Sodium . . . . . . 237 mg	
Carbohydrate . . . . 50 g	
Dietary Fiber . . . . . 4 g	
Sugars . . . . 6 g	
Protein . . . . 26 g	

2 Tbsp canola oil
1 garlic clove, minced
1 medium onion, chopped
2 small zucchini, julienned
1/2 small red or yellow pepper, julienned
2 small ripe plum tomatoes, diced
1 cup frozen peas, thawed
1/4 cup chopped fresh dill
2 Tbsp tarragon
3 Tbsp fresh lemon juice
1 1/2 lb peeled and deveined medium shrimp
1/4 tsp red pepper flakes
Fresh ground pepper and salt to taste
6 cups cooked small shells, radiatore, or penne

1. Heat the oil in a large skillet or wok over medium heat. Add the garlic and onion and saute for 1 minute. Add the zucchini and pepper and saute for 1 more minute.
2. Add all remaining ingredients except the pasta and stir well. Cover and bring to a boil. Reduce heat and simmer for 2 minutes. Add the pasta and stir thoroughly.

Preparation time: 20 minutes

Three Mushroom Stroganoff

12 Servings/Serving Size:
1/2 cup pasta with 1/2 cup stroganoff

Exchanges:

2 1/2	Starch
2	Very Lean Meat

Calories 258	
Calories from Fat . . 18	
Total Fat . . . . 2 g	
Saturated Fat . . . . 0 g	

Cholesterol . . . . 73 mg	
Sodium. . . . . . 102 mg	
Carbohydrate. . . . 34 g	
Dietary Fiber. . . . . 2 g	
Sugars . . . . 5 g	

Protein . . . . 23 g	

Preparation time: 20 minutes

10 dried shiitake mushrooms
15 dried porcini mushrooms
10 fresh white mushrooms or cremini mushrooms
1 cup dry white wine
1 medium onion, diced
2 garlic cloves, minced
1 tsp paprika
1 1/2 lb cooked ground turkey
1 1/4 cups low-fat, low-sodium chicken broth
2 Tbsp cornstarch or arrowroot powder
4 Tbsp water
2 cups nonfat sour cream
1/4 cup chopped scallions
1 Tbsp minced fresh parsley
6 cups cooked wide noodles

1. Rehydrate the shiitake and porcini mushrooms by pouring boiling water over them in a heatproof bowl. Let stand at room temperature for 20 minutes. Drain. Take stems off shiitake mushrooms and slice. Leave the porcini mushrooms whole. Stem and slice the fresh mushrooms. Heat the wine in a large nonstick skillet. Add the mushrooms, onion, garlic, and paprika and cook for 8 minutes.
2. Add the turkey and cook for 2 minutes. Add in the broth and bring to a boil. Lower the heat. Mix together the cornstarch or arrowroot powder and water and add to the skillet. Cook until thickened. Remove from the heat. Add in the sour cream, scallions, and parsley. Serve the stroganoff over cooked, hot noodles.

Turkey Tetrazzini

Use that leftover holiday turkey in this creamy dish.

6 Servings/Serving Size: 1 cup	
Exchanges:	
2	Starch
1	Vegetable
1	Lean Meat

Calories	243
Calories from Fat	37
Total Fat	4 g
Saturated Fat	2 g

Cholesterol	19 mg
Sodium	154 mg
Carbohydrate	35 g
Dietary Fiber	2 g
Sugars	9 g

Protein	17 g

Preparation time: 20 minutes

1 Tbsp low-calorie margarine
2 cups sliced mushrooms
2 Tbsp unbleached white flour
1 tsp paprika
2 cups evaporated fat-free milk
1/4 cup grated Swiss cheese
1/2 cup sliced scallions
1/4 cup diced red pepper
1/2 cup diced turkey
1 lb cooked thin spaghetti
1 Tbsp grated Parmesan cheese

1. Preheat the oven to 350 degrees. Melt the margarine in a heavy skillet over medium-high heat. Add the mushrooms and saute for 5 minutes. Sprinkle the flour and paprika over the mushrooms. Add the milk and stir until thickened.

2. Add the remaining ingredients except the Parmesan cheese. Pour the mixture into a 2-quart casserole dish. Sprinkle with the Parmesan cheese. Bake for 15 minutes until bubbly.

Seafood

Chunky Lobster Rolls

You can also try cooked jumbo shrimp in these tasty pita sandwiches. (This recipe is relatively high in sodium.)

6 Servings/Serving Size: 3 oz	
Exchanges:	
2 1/2	Starch
3	Very Lean Meat
Calories 294	
Calories from Fat . . 32	
Total Fat . . . . 4 g	
Saturated Fat . . . . 0 g	
Cholesterol . . . . 82 mg	
Sodium . . . . . . 758 mg	
Carbohydrate . . . . 39 g	
Dietary Fiber . . . . . 3 g	
Sugars . . . . 8 g	
Protein . . . . 30 g	

1 1/2 lb cooked lobster meat, cartilage removed
3 garlic cloves, minced
1/2 cup low-fat mayonnaise
1/2 cup sliced celery
1/2 cup minced scallions
1 Tbsp lemon juice
1 cup shredded romaine lettuce
6 whole-wheat pita bread halves or whole-grain hamburger rolls

1. Mix together the cooked lobster with all ingredients except the lettuce and bread. If using pita bread, stuff the mixture and the lettuce into the pocket and serve.
2. If using hamburger rolls, scoop out some of the bread on one side of each roll to form a pocket. Place shredded lettuce in the hole. Pile on the lobster salad and top with remaining roll half.

Preparation time: 15 minutes

Citrus Swordfish with Tropical Salsa

This salsa is great served with any grilled fish or chicken. Try doubling this recipe and using the leftovers in Citrus Swordfish Salad (see recipe, p. 35).

6 Servings/Serving Size: 3–4 oz	
Exchanges:	
1	Fruit
3	Very Lean Meat
1/2 Monounsaturated Fat	
Calories 195	
Calories from Fat . . 52	
Total Fat . . . . 6 g	
Saturated Fat . . . . 1 g	
Cholesterol . . . . 44 mg	
Sodium . . . . . 104 mg	
Carbohydrate . . . . 12 g	
Dietary Fiber . . . . . 1 g	
Sugars . . . . 10 g	
Protein . . . . 23 g	

Swordfish
1 1/2 lb swordfish steaks
1/2 cup fresh orange juice
1 Tbsp olive oil
1/4 tsp cayenne pepper
1 Tbsp pineapple juice concentrate

Salsa
1 medium orange, peeled, sectioned, and chopped into 1-inch pieces
1/2 cup diced pineapple chunks (use either fresh or packed in their own juice, juice drained)
1/4 cup diced mango
2 jalapeno peppers, minced
3 Tbsp orange juice
1 Tbsp diced red pepper
2 tsp sugar
1 Tbsp minced cilantro

Preparation time: 25 minutes

1. Using a glass or ceramic bowl, marinate the swordfish in the orange juice, olive oil, cayenne pepper, and pineapple juice concentrate for 30 minutes. Prepare an outside grill with an oiled rack set 6 inches above the heat source. On a gas grill, set the heat to medium.
2. Grill the swordfish for about 6–7 minutes on each side until the swordfish is opaque in the center. Combine all ingredients for the salsa and serve it with the grilled swordfish.

Grilled Red Snapper with Vera Cruz Sauce

Moist red snapper is livened up with a chili-spiked tomato sauce.

6 Servings/Serving Size: 3–4 oz with sauce

Exchanges:

2	Vegetable
3	Very Lean Meat
1/2	Monounsaturated Fat

Calories	173
Calories from Fat	45
Total Fat	5 g
Saturated Fat	1 g
Cholesterol	41 mg
Sodium	140 mg
Carbohydrate	8 g
Dietary Fiber	2 g
Sugars	4 g
Protein	24 g

Preparation time: 25 minutes

1 1/2 lb red snapper filets
2 tsp chili powder
2 tsp olive oil
Fresh ground pepper to taste
2 tsp olive oil
1/2 cup minced onion
2 garlic cloves, minced
3 medium tomatoes, seeded and diced
1/4 cup fresh lime juice
2 tsp cinnamon
1 can (4 1/2 oz) green chilies
Fresh ground white pepper to taste

1. Rub the red snapper filets with the chili powder and olive oil. Grind black pepper over each filet. Let sit for 30 minutes. Heat the oil in a medium skillet over medium-high heat. Add the onion and garlic and saute for 3–4 minutes.
2. Add the diced tomatoes and lime juice. Bring to a boil, lower the heat, and simmer for 10 minutes. Add the cinnamon, green chilies, and white pepper and simmer for 5 minutes. Keep sauce on low heat.
3. Prepare an outside grill with an oiled rack set 6 inches above the heat source. On a gas grill, set the heat to medium. Grill the red snapper filets for 5 minutes on each side, turning once. Serve the filets with the Vera Cruz sauce on the side.

Grilled Salmon with Rigatoni and Herbed Tomato Relish

Use this tasty relish to top grilled chicken, too.

6 Servings/Serving Size:
3 oz salmon with 1 cup pasta

Exchanges:

2 1/2	Starch
1	Vegetable
3	Very Lean Meat
1/2	Fat

Calories	356
Calories from Fat	62
Total Fat	7 g
Saturated Fat	2 g
Cholesterol	43 mg
Sodium	90 mg
Carbohydrate	39 g
Dietary Fiber	3 g
Sugars	5 g
Protein	33 g

1 1/2 lb fresh boneless salmon (you can also try tuna or monkfish)
4 large, ripe tomatoes, chopped
1 cup fresh basil leaves
1/2 cup fresh mint leaves
1 Tbsp lemon juice
Fresh ground pepper and salt to taste
6 cups cooked rigatoni pasta

1. Prepare an outside grill with an oiled rack set 4 inches above the heat source. On a gas grill, set the heat to high.
2. Grill the salmon until it flakes easily, turning once, for a total of about 10 minutes. Combine the remaining ingredients in a bowl, toss lightly with the salmon, and serve.

Preparation time: 20 minutes

Grilled Salmon with Yogurt Dill Sauce

The flavors of sour cream, yogurt, and dill enhance fresh grilled salmon.

6 Servings/Serving Size: 3–4 oz with 2 1/2 Tbsp sauce

Exchanges:

1/2	Starch
3	Lean Meat
1/2 Monounsaturated Fat	

Calories	241
Calories from Fat	106
Total Fat	12 g
Saturated Fat	2 g
Cholesterol	79 mg
Sodium	101 mg
Carbohydrate	5 g
Dietary Fiber	0 g
Sugars	3 g
Protein	26 g

1 1/2 lb salmon filets
1 Tbsp olive oil
2 Tbsp lemon juice
1 Tbsp minced fresh parsley
1/2 cup nonfat sour cream
1/2 cup plain low-fat yogurt
2 tsp sherry vinegar
1 Tbsp minced fresh dill
1 Tbsp minced scallions

1. Marinate the salmon in the oil, lemon juice, and parsley for 30 minutes. Prepare an outside grill with an oiled rack set 6 inches above the heat source. On a gas grill, set the heat to medium.
2. Grill the salmon for about 4–5 minutes on each side. Combine all ingredients for the sauce and serve it with the grilled salmon.

Preparation time: 20 minutes

Grilled Shrimp with Pasta and Pineapple Salsa

This is a light, refreshing main course with a tang of citrus.

6 Servings/Serving Size:
3 oz shrimp with 1 cup pasta

Exchanges:

3 1/2	Starch
3	Very Lean Meat

Calories	383
Calories from Fat	30
Total Fat	3 g
Saturated Fat	1 g

Cholesterol	170 mg
Sodium	170 mg
Carbohydrate	57 g
Dietary Fiber	4 g
Sugars	14 g

Protein	31 g

2 15-oz cans pineapple chunks, packed in their own juice, drained
1 large red pepper, chopped
1 large red onion, chopped
1 jalapeno pepper, minced
1/2 cup orange juice
1/3 cup lime juice
1 1/2 lb peeled and deveined large shrimp
6 cups cooked rotini pasta

1. In a large bowl, combine all salsa ingredients except the shrimp and pasta. Prepare an outside grill with an oiled rack set 4 inches above the heat source. On a gas grill, set the heat to high.
2. Grill the shrimp on each side for 2 minutes. Toss the pasta with the salsa, arrange the shrimp on top, and serve.

Preparation time: 20 minutes

Grilled Tuna with Chinese Five Spice Sauce

You can find Chinese Five Spice in the Asian section of your grocery store or in a specialty market. (This recipe is high in sodium.)

6 Servings/Serving Size: 3–4 oz	
Exchanges:	
1	Starch
3	Very Lean Meat
1/2	Fat
Calories 218	
Calories from Fat . . 58	
Total Fat . . . . 6 g	
Saturated Fat . . . . 2 g	
Cholesterol . . . . 42 mg	
Sodium . . . . . 1264 mg	
Carbohydrate . . . . 12 g	
Dietary Fiber . . . . . 1 g	
Sugars . . . . 10 g	
Protein . . . . 27 g	

1 1/2 lb tuna steaks
2 tsp sesame oil
2 Tbsp lemon juice
1/2 cup lite soy sauce
1/2 cup Hoisin sauce
1 Tbsp honey
2 garlic cloves, minced
2 tsp Chinese Five Spice

1. Marinate the tuna steaks in the sesame oil and lemon juice for 30 minutes. Prepare an outside grill with an oiled rack set 6 inches above the heat source. On a gas grill, set the heat to medium.
2. While the tuna steaks are marinating, combine the remaining sauce ingredients and heat in a pan for 10 minutes over medium heat.
3. Grill the tuna steaks for 6–7 minutes on each side, turning once, basting each side occasionally with the sauce. (Cook for a few minutes less if you like your tuna a little rarer.) Serve the tuna steaks with any remaining sauce on the side.

Preparation time: 20 minutes

Herbed Crab Sandwiches

Crab and cream cheese are a great combination. (These sandwiches are relatively high in sodium.)

6 Servings/Serving Size:
1 English muffin,
3 oz crab

Exchanges:

2	Starch
3	Lean Meat

Calories 326
  Calories from Fat . . 97
Total Fat . . . . 11 g
  Saturated Fat . . . . 5 g

Cholesterol . . . 163 mg
Sodium . . . . . . 703 mg
Carbohydrate . . . . 32 g
  Dietary Fiber . . . . . 2 g
  Sugars . . . . 7 g

Protein . . . . 24 g

1 1/2 lb lump crabmeat
1/4 cup low-fat mayonnaise
1 Tbsp minced fresh parsley
1 Tbsp minced fresh tarragon
2 Tbsp minced scallions
6 oz low-fat cream cheese
2 eggs, beaten
1 tsp Dijon mustard
6 English muffins, split and toasted
6 slices tomato

1. Combine the crab, mayonnaise, parsley, tarragon, and scallions in a medium bowl. In a separate bowl, beat together the cream cheese, eggs, and mustard. Spread the crab mixture over the English muffins.
2. Spread the cream cheese mixture on top, and broil the muffins 6 inches from the heat source for 3 minutes. Add the tomato slices and broil again for 2 more minutes.

Preparation time: 15 minutes

Italian Grilled Tuna

Red peppers give this fresh tuna a festive look.

6 Servings/Serving Size: 3–4 oz	
Exchanges:	
4	Lean Meat
Calories 237	
Calories from Fat . . 94	
Total Fat . . . . 10 g	
Saturated Fat . . . . 3 g	
Cholesterol . . . . 69 mg	
Sodium . . . . . 52 mg	
Carbohydrate . . . . . 3 g	
Dietary Fiber. . . . . 0 g	
Sugars . . . . 2 g	
Protein . . . . 25 g	

1 1/2 lb tuna steaks
2 Tbsp fresh lemon juice
1/2 cup diced roasted red peppers
1/2 cup sliced scallions
2 Tbsp minced fresh oregano
2 Tbsp minced fresh Italian parsley
1/3 cup balsamic vinegar
1 Tbsp olive oil
Fresh ground pepper and salt to taste

1. Combine the tuna steaks and lemon juice and marinate for 15 minutes. Prepare an outside grill with an oiled rack set 6 inches above the heat source. On a gas grill, set the heat to medium.
2. Grill or broil the tuna 6 inches from the heat source for 4–5 minutes on each side. Combine all remaining ingredients in a saucepan and bring to a boil. Pour the sauce over the tuna steaks to serve.

Preparation time: 15 minutes

Mussels au Gratin

Cracker crumbs and Parmesan cheese make these mussels golden and crusty!

6 Servings/Serving Size: 3–4 oz		
Exchanges:		
1		Starch
2		Very Lean Meat
1		Monounsaturated Fat
Calories 190		
Calories from Fat . . 80		
Total Fat . . . . 9 g		
Saturated Fat . . . . 2 g		
Cholesterol . . . . 27 mg		
Sodium . . . . . . 467 mg		
Carbohydrate . . . . 13 g		
Dietary Fiber . . . . . 1 g		
Sugars . . . . 4 g		
Protein . . . . 13 g		

4 lb mussels
1/2 cup water
4 cloves garlic, minced
1 tsp ground pepper
2 Tbsp olive oil
3 Tbsp white wine
1/4 cup finely diced onion
1/2 cup finely minced fresh parsley
2 Tbsp fresh lemon juice
1 cup cracker crumbs
1/4 cup Parmesan cheese

Preparation time: 25 minutes

1. Preheat the oven to 400 degrees. Scrub the mussels under running water; discard any that are not closed. Cut off beards (or you can have your seafood department do this for you). In a large pot, combine water, half of the garlic, and half of the pepper. Bring to a boil. Add the mussels and steam on medium heat until they open, about 7–10 minutes.

2. With a slotted spoon, transfer the mussels from the broth onto 2 rimmed baking sheets. Break off and discard the top halves of the shells and any unopened mussels. Heat the olive oil and wine in a medium skillet. Saute the remaining garlic and onion for 5 minutes. Add the parsley, lemon juice, and remaining pepper. Combine with the cracker crumbs and Parmesan cheese. Sprinkle the mixture over the mussels. Bake the mussels for 5 minutes until crumbs are lightly browned.

This recipe is courtesy of the National Fisheries Institute.

Orange-Glazed Swordfish

These moist swordfish steaks are scented with ginger.

6 Servings/Serving Size:
3–4 oz

Exchanges:

3	Very Lean Meat
1	Fat

Calories	167
Calories from Fat	55
Total Fat	6 g
Saturated Fat	1 g

Cholesterol	44 mg
Sodium	304 mg
Carbohydrate	4 g
Dietary Fiber	0 g
Sugars	3 g

Protein	23 g

Preparation time: 10 minutes

1 1/2 lb fresh swordfish steaks
1/2 cup fresh orange juice
1 Tbsp grated fresh ginger
2 tsp sesame oil
2 Tbsp lite soy sauce
1 Tbsp cornstarch or arrowroot powder
2 Tbsp water

1. Combine the swordfish with the orange juice, ginger, sesame oil, and soy sauce and marinate for 30 minutes. Prepare an outside grill with an oiled rack set 6 inches above the heat source. On a gas grill, set the heat to medium.
2. Drain and reserve the marinade. Grill the swordfish for about 6–7 minutes on each side until the swordfish is opaque in the center.
3. Place the reserved marinade in a saucepan and bring to a boil. Mix together the cornstarch or arrowroot powder with the water. Add to the sauce and cook for 1 more minute until thickened. Serve the orange sauce with the swordfish steaks.

Scallop and Shrimp Kabobs

It is important not to overcook small pieces of shellfish like shrimp and scallops. Cook just until scallops turn opaque and shrimp turns pink, and immediately remove the kabob from the heat.

6 Servings/Serving Size:
3–4 oz seafood plus vegetables and fruit

Exchanges:

1/2	Fruit
1	Vegetable
2	Very Lean Meat

Calories	123
Calories from Fat	20
Total Fat	2 g
Saturated Fat	0 g
Cholesterol	118 mg
Sodium	403 mg
Carbohydrate	10 g
Dietary Fiber	1g
Sugars	7 g
Protein	17 g

Preparation time: 20 minutes

1 lb shelled, peeled large shrimp
  (keep tails on)
1/2 lb scallops
1 medium red pepper, cut into 1-inch pieces
1 medium green pepper, cut into
  1-inch pieces
12 2-inch wedges of fresh pineapple
1/2 cup rice vinegar
2 tsp sesame oil
2 tsp minced ginger
3 Tbsp lite soy sauce

1. If using wooden kabob skewers, soak 6 of them in warm water for 15 minutes. This prevents the skewers from catching on fire while the kabobs cook. Then thread the shrimp, scallops, peppers, and pineapple on the skewers.
2. Prepare an outside grill with an oiled rack set 4 inches above the heat source. On a gas grill, set the heat to high. Combine all remaining ingredients for the basting sauce. Place the skewers on the grill and baste with some of the sauce.
3. Grill kabobs for about 5–6 minutes total, turning and basting with the sauce while grilling. Heat remaining basting sauce until warm and serve on the side.

Scallops with Tarragon Mustard Sauce

This subtle sauce is a great complement to the flavor of fresh scallops.

6 Servings/Serving Size: 3 oz	
Exchanges:	
1/2	Starch
1	Fat-Free Milk
3	Very Lean Meat
Calories 245	
Calories from Fat . . 38	
Total Fat . . . . 4 g	
Saturated Fat . . . . 2 g	
Cholesterol . . . . 47 mg	
Sodium . . . . . . 611 mg	
Carbohydrate . . . . 20 g	
Dietary Fiber. . . . . 0 g	
Sugars . . . . 15 g	
Protein . . . . 30 g	

1/2 cup dry white wine
1/2 cup low-fat, low-sodium chicken broth
2 shallots, minced
2 12-oz cans evaporated fat-free milk
1/4 cup smooth Dijon mustard
1/4 cup coarse Dijon mustard
1 Tbsp butter
1 1/2 lb sea scallops
1/4 cup finely minced fresh parsley

1. In a skillet over medium-high heat, heat the wine, broth, and shallots until the liquid is reduced by one-third. Add the milk, lower the heat, and reduce again by one-third. Add the mustard and stir until smooth. Do not boil.
2. In another skillet, melt the butter. Add the scallops and cook about 3–4 minutes until scallops turn opaque. Place the scallops on plates and spoon the sauce over them. Garnish with parsley.

Preparation time: 35 minutes

Stuffed Whole Trout

Leave the head and tail on your trout for an authentic look. The seafood department at the grocery store will clean and scale your fish for you.

6 Servings/Serving Size: 3–4 oz

Exchanges:
1/2 Starch
2 Medium-Fat Meat

Calories	184
Calories from Fat	90
Total Fat	10 g
Saturated Fat	2 g
Cholesterol	46 mg
Sodium	87 mg
Carbohydrate	5 g
Dietary Fiber	0 g
Sugars	1 g
Protein	17 g

1 3-lb whole trout, cleaned, scaled, and slit open to form a pocket
2 cups soft bread crumbs
2 Tbsp olive oil
1 small onion, minced
1 Tbsp minced fresh dill

1. Prepare an outside grill with an oiled rack set 6 inches above the heat source. On a gas grill, set the heat to medium. Rinse the fish inside and out with cool water. Pat dry. In a bowl, combine the remaining ingredients. Stuff the bread mixture into the cavity of the fish.
2. Either place the fish in an oiled fish basket and cook for about 25–30 minutes, turning every 10 minutes, or wrap the entire fish in a double thickness of aluminum foil and grill for 30–40 minutes, turning every 10 minutes.
3. To serve, unwrap the fish from the foil or remove carefully from the basket. Place on a platter, remove the skin, and cut the fish into pieces. You may save the bones for making fish stock if you wish.

Preparation time: 15 minutes

Poultry

Allan's Cranberry Chicken

This dish is great served with rice.

6 Servings/Serving Size: 3–4 oz	

Exchanges:

1/2	Carbohydrate
1	Vegetable
3	Very Lean Meat
1/2	Fat

Calories	196
Calories from Fat	41
Total Fat	5 g
Saturated Fat	1 g

Cholesterol	69 mg
Sodium	76 mg
Carbohydrate	12 g
Dietary Fiber	2 g
Sugars	9 g

Protein	26 g

Preparation time: 15 minutes

1 cup boiling water
1/2 cup dried cranberries
2 tsp canola oil
1 1/2 lb skinless, boneless chicken breasts, halved and pounded to 1/2-inch thickness
1 large carrot, peeled and diagonally sliced
1 red pepper, julienned
1 yellow pepper, julienned
2 scallions, sliced
2 Tbsp honey
1 Tbsp lemon juice

1. Pour the boiling water over the cranberries and set aside. Heat the oil in a large skillet over medium-high heat. Add the chicken breasts and saute on each side for a total of 10 minutes. Remove from the skillet.
2. Add the carrot and peppers and saute for 5 minutes. Add the scallions and saute for 3 more minutes.
3. Mix together the honey and lemon juice. Add the cranberries (do not drain) and the juice mixture to the skillet and cook 1 minute. Add the chicken breasts, cover, and simmer on low for 5 minutes.

Best Oven-Fried Chicken

All the crunch of good fried chicken without the fat!

6 Servings/Serving Size: 3–4 oz	
Exchanges:	
1	Starch
4	Lean Meat
Calories 311	
Calories from Fat . 120	
Total Fat . . . . 13 g	
Saturated Fat . . . . 3 g	
Cholesterol . . . 142 mg	
Sodium . . . . . . 343 mg	
Carbohydrate . . . . 14 g	
Dietary Fiber . . . . . 1 g	
Sugars . . . . 1 g	
Protein . . . . 32 g	

Preparation time: 15 minutes

1 cup bread crumbs
1/4 cup Parmesan cheese
1 tsp garlic powder
1 tsp onion powder
1 tsp minced fresh thyme
1/2 tsp minced fresh oregano
1 tsp minced fresh basil
2 tsp paprika
Fresh ground pepper and salt to taste
2 eggs
2 egg whites
1 tsp hot pepper sauce
1 1/2 lb boneless, skinless chicken breasts, halved
3 Tbsp olive oil

1. Preheat the oven to 350 degrees. Combine the bread crumbs, Parmesan cheese, and spices in a plastic bag. In a shallow bowl, beat the eggs and egg whites. Add the hot pepper sauce. Dip each chicken breast into beaten eggs. Roll in the bread crumb mixture.

2. Spread the chicken breasts out on a cookie sheet. Drizzle olive oil on each chicken breast. Bake the chicken for 30–35 minutes until no traces of pink remain.

Chicken Caesar Salad Sandwiches

This is a healthy alternative to sandwiches made with processed meats.

6 Servings/Serving Size: 1 3-oz roll with 3 oz chicken and 1/2 cup salad greens	
Exchanges:	
3	Starch
4	Very Lean Meat
1/2	Fat
Calories	401
Calories from Fat . .	84
Total Fat	9 g
Saturated Fat	3 g
Cholesterol	72 mg
Sodium.	793 mg
Carbohydrate. . . .	44 g
Dietary Fiber.	7 g
Sugars	5 g
Protein	36 g

6 medium hard rolls (preferably whole grain)
3 cups torn romaine lettuce
1/2 cup fat-free Caesar salad dressing
1/3 cup grated fresh Parmesan cheese
1 1/2 lb chicken breasts, cut into strips about
   3 inches long
2 tsp olive oil

1. Set the oven on broil. Cut each roll in half and scoop out the dough in one side of the bread to form a pocket. Combine the lettuce, dressing, and cheese in a bowl.
2. Place the chicken strips on a broiler pan and brush with the olive oil. Broil the strips of chicken for a total of about 7 minutes, turning once. Add the chicken to the salad and pile the mixture into the bread pocket. Top with the other half of bread and serve.

Preparation time: 15 minutes

Chicken Jubilee

Dark cherries give this dish its eye appeal.

6 Servings/Serving Size: 3–4 oz	
Exchanges:	
1	Fruit
4	Very Lean Meat
Calories 208	
Calories from Fat . . 48	
Total Fat . . . . 5 g	
Saturated Fat . . . . 1 g	
Cholesterol . . . . 69 mg	
Sodium . . . . . . 258 mg	
Carbohydrate . . . . 11 g	
Dietary Fiber . . . . . 0 g	
Sugars . . . . 6 g	
Protein . . . . 26 g	

1 1/2 lb chicken cutlets
1/4 cup unbleached flour
1/2 tsp salt
1/2 tsp pepper
2 tsp canola oil
1 9-oz can dark cherries in water (reserve juice)
1 Tbsp cherry preserves
3 Tbsp brandy

1. In a plastic bag, combine the chicken cutlets with the flour, salt, and pepper. Shake to coat well. Heat the oil in a skillet over medium-high heat.
2. Add the chicken cutlets and cook on each side for about 4–5 minutes. Remove the chicken from the skillet.
3. Add the cherries, cherry juice, preserves, and brandy to the skillet. Bring to a boil and boil 1 minute. Spoon the cherry juice over the chicken and serve.

Preparation time: 15 minutes

Chicken Nuggets

These nuggets are easy finger food to eat without fuss.

6 Servings/Serving Size: 3 oz	
Exchanges:	
1	Starch
4	Very Lean Meat
1/2	Monounsaturated Fat

Calories	 239
Calories from Fat	. . 64
Total Fat	. . . . 7 g
Saturated Fat	. . . . 2 g
Cholesterol	. . . . 71 mg
Sodium	. . . . . 275 mg
Carbohydrate	. . . . 13 g
Dietary Fiber	. . . . . 1 g
Sugars	. . . . 1 g
Protein	. . . . 29 g

1 cup dry bread crumbs
1/4 cup Parmesan cheese
2 tsp dried oregano
2 tsp dried basil
1 tsp paprika
1/2 tsp dried thyme
1 1/2 lb boneless, skinless chicken breasts, cut into 2-inch cubes
1 Tbsp olive oil

1. Preheat the oven to 350 degrees. Combine all ingredients except chicken and oil in a plastic bag. Place chicken cubes in the bag and shake well.
2. Place the cubes on a nonstick cookie sheet. Drizzle olive oil over the cubes, or mist lightly with olive oil from a spray bottle. Bake the cubes for about 10 minutes until chicken is cooked through and tender. Serve cold.

Preparation time: 10 minutes

Corn Tortilla Turkey Pizzas

This is a great low-fat Mexican food and pizza combination!

6 Servings/Serving Size: 1 tortilla pizza	
Exchanges:	
1	Starch
1	Vegetable
2	Lean Meat

Calories	220
Calories from Fat	62
Total Fat	7 g
Saturated Fat	2 g

Cholesterol	44 mg
Sodium	399 mg
Carbohydrate	19 g
Dietary Fiber	4 g
Sugars	4 g

Protein	19 g

1 Tbsp olive oil
12 oz ground turkey (have your butcher grind this for you)
1 cup finely diced zucchini
1 cup finely diced red pepper
2 tsp minced fresh oregano
1 tsp minced fresh basil
6 6-inch corn tortillas (yellow or blue)
1 1/2 cups marinara sauce
1/4 cup sliced black olives
1/2 cup part-skim mozzarella cheese

1. Preheat the oven to 350 degrees. Heat the oil in a skillet over medium-high heat. Add the ground turkey and saute for 3 minutes. Add the zucchini and red pepper and continue to cook until the turkey is cooked through, about 3–4 minutes. Add the oregano and basil.
2. To assemble the pizzas, spoon some of the sauce over each tortilla. Add the turkey mixture. Dot with olives and sprinkle with cheese. Place the pizzas on a baking sheet and bake until the cheese melts and the tortilla is crisp, about 5–6 minutes.

Preparation time: 15 minutes

*I*talian Turkey Saute

Be sure to use cooked turkey within a week for safety and best freshness. To freeze cooked turkey, wrap large pieces in plastic wrap, then in butcher paper or foil.

6 Servings/Serving Size:
3–4 oz

Exchanges:

1	Vegetable
3	Very Lean Meat
1/2	Fat

Calories	159
Calories from Fat	35
Total Fat	4 g
Saturated Fat	1 g
Cholesterol	49 mg
Sodium	217 mg
Carbohydrate	7 g
Dietary Fiber	2 g
Sugars	4 g
Protein	23 g

2 tsp olive oil
1/2 cup diced onion
2 garlic cloves, minced
1 1/2 cups crushed tomatoes
2 Tbsp red wine
2 tsp minced fresh oregano
3 cups leftover, cubed cooked turkey
  (preferably white meat)
2 Tbsp minced fresh basil
2 Tbsp capers

1. Heat the oil in a large skillet over medium-high heat. Add the onion and saute for 5 minutes. Add the garlic and saute for 2 more minutes.
2. Add the crushed tomatoes and wine. Bring to a boil. Lower the heat and simmer for 10 minutes. Add the remaining ingredients and simmer for 5 minutes.

Preparation time: 15 minutes

Low-Fat Chicken Tostadas

Serve these tasty tostadas with some black bean soup and a chilled fruit dessert!

6 Servings/Serving Size:
3–4 oz chicken

Exchanges:

1 1/2	Starch
1	Vegetable
4	Very Lean Meat

Calories	292
Calories from Fat	57
Total Fat	6 g
Saturated Fat	2 g
Cholesterol	76 mg
Sodium	309 mg
Carbohydrate	23 g
Dietary Fiber	3 g
Sugars	4 g
Protein	33 g

1 1/2 lb cooked, boneless, skinless chicken breast, shredded
3 cups shredded romaine lettuce
1/2 cup chopped red pepper
1/2 cup chopped green pepper
1/2 cup chopped fresh tomatoes
6 6-in flour tortillas
6 Tbsp fat-free sour cream
6 Tbsp salsa
6 Tbsp low-fat cheddar cheese

1. Combine the chicken, lettuce, peppers, tomatoes, and onions in a large bowl. Heat the tortillas by placing them one at a time in a dry skillet and turning once until brown and puffy.
2. To assemble the tostadas, place a tortilla on a plate, top with some of the chicken mixture, and garnish with sour cream, salsa, and cheese.

Preparation time: 15 minutes

Orange-Grilled Chicken with Herbs

Tucking fresh herbs under the skin of the chicken adds a wonderful flavor.

6 Servings/Serving Size:
3–4 oz chicken
without skin

Exchanges:
4   Very Lean Meat

Calories 138
  Calories from Fat . . 26
Total Fat . . . . 3 g
  Saturated Fat . . . . 1 g

Cholesterol . . . . 69 mg
Sodium . . . . . . 66 mg
Carbohydrate . . . . . 1 g
  Dietary Fiber . . . . . 0 g
  Sugars . . . . 1 g

Protein . . . . 25 g

2 garlic cloves, minced
1 tsp grated orange peel
1/2 tsp minced fresh thyme
1/2 tsp minced fresh rosemary
Fresh ground pepper to taste
1 1/2 lb boneless chicken breasts, skin attached
1/2 cup fresh orange juice
2 Tbsp vinegar
1 Tbsp Worcestershire sauce

1. Combine the first five ingredients in a small bowl to make the herb mixture. Take each chicken breast and slip your fingers between the skin and flesh of the chicken, leaving the skin attached. Slide some of the herb mixture under the skin of each breast, pulling the skin back over each breast when finished.
2. Prepare an outside grill with an oiled rack set 4 inches above the heat source. On a gas grill, set the heat to high. Mix together the orange juice, vinegar, and Worcestershire sauce in a small bowl.
3. Grill the chicken breasts for 3–4 minutes on each side, turning once and basting with the orange juice mixture, until the chicken is cooked through. Remove the skin before eating.

This adapted recipe is courtesy of the National Broiler Council.

Pita Pizza Pizzazz

Kids love to help make these pita pizzas.

6 Servings/Serving Size:
1 oz bread with
2 oz meat and
1/2 cup vegetables

Exchanges:

1	Starch
2	Vegetable
3	Very Lean Meat
1/2	Fat

Calories	258
Calories from Fat	56
Total Fat	6 g
Saturated Fat	3 g

Cholesterol	54 mg
Sodium	499 mg
Carbohydrate	23 g
Dietary Fiber	4 g
Sugars	5 g

Protein	26 g

3 whole-wheat pita breads, split
1 1/2 cups marinara sauce
1 Tbsp olive oil
1 cup sliced zucchini
1 cup chopped broccoli
1 cup diced red peppers
3/4 lb ground turkey (have your butcher grind this for you)
6 oz part-skim mozzarella cheese

1. Preheat the oven to 350 degrees. Spread some of the marinara sauce on each pita bread pizza. Place all pizzas on a cookie sheet. Heat the oil in a small skillet over medium-high heat. Add the zucchini, broccoli, and peppers and saute for 10 minutes.

2. Remove the vegetables from the skillet and place on all the pizzas. In the same skillet, brown the turkey meat until no pink remains. Divide the turkey evenly over each pizza. Sprinkle cheese on each pizza and bake for 5 minutes until the cheese melts.

Preparation time: 10 minutes

Steamed Chicken with Chinese Barbecue Sauce

Steaming is the best way to keep fat at bay!

6 Servings/Serving Size:
3–4 oz

Exchanges:
4   Very Lean Meat

Calories 151
  Calories from Fat . . 28
Total Fat . . . . 3 g
  Saturated Fat . . . . 1 g

Cholesterol . . . . 69 mg
Sodium. . . . . . 374 mg
Carbohydrate. . . . . 4 g
  Dietary Fiber. . . . . 0 g
  Sugars . . . . 4 g

Protein . . . . 25 g

Preparation time: 10 minutes

1 1/2 lb skinless, boneless chicken breasts, halved and pounded to 1/2-inch thickness
2 Tbsp lite soy sauce
1 Tbsp minced ginger
1/2 cup rice vinegar
1/3 cup barbecue sauce
2 garlic cloves, minced
1/2 tsp Chinese Five Spice
1/2 cup minced scallions

1. Arrange the chicken breasts on a heatproof plate. Sprinkle the chicken with soy sauce and ginger. Place a metal rack inside a deep wok, set the wok to high, and add 2–3 inches of water to the bottom of the wok.
2. Place the plate of chicken on the rack, cover the wok, and steam the chicken for about 10–15 minutes, adding more water if necessary. (No trace of pink should remain. You may need to steam the chicken in two batches.)
3. While the chicken is steaming, heat the remaining ingredients except the scallions in a saucepan over medium heat. Remove the steamed chicken from the wok and garnish chicken with scallions. Serve with hot barbecue sauce on the side.

Beef, Pork, & Lamb

Garlic-Stuffed Sirloin Steak

The flavors of mellow garlic and juicy beef mingle in every bite!

6 Servings/Serving Size: 3–4 oz	
Exchanges:	
4	Lean Meat
Calories	220
Calories from Fat . .	80
Total Fat	9 g
Saturated Fat	3 g
Cholesterol	88 mg
Sodium	91 mg
Carbohydrate.	3 g
Dietary Fiber.	0 g
Sugars	2 g
Protein	31 g

Preparation time: 20 minutes

1 Tbsp olive oil
1/4 cup finely chopped garlic
1/2 cup minced scallions
Fresh ground pepper and salt to taste
2 1/2 lb boneless top sirloin steak,
   cut 2 inches thick

1. Heat the oil in a medium skillet over medium heat. Add the garlic and saute for 5 minutes. Add the scallions and cook for 5 more minutes. Add the pepper and salt. Remove from the heat and let cool. Prepare an outside grill with an oiled rack set 6 inches above the heat source. On a gas grill, set the heat to medium.
2. Trim the excess fat from the steak. Make a horizontal slice through the center of the steak, parallel to the surface of the meat, about 1 inch from each side. Cut to, but not through, the opposite side. Spoon the stuffing into the pocket, spreading evenly. Secure the opening with toothpicks.
3. Grill the steak, turning once, according to the following guidelines: 15–20 minutes for rare, 25–30 minutes for medium, or 35–40 minutes for well done. Remove the toothpicks and slice to serve.

This adapted recipe is courtesy of the Beef Board and Veal Committee/ Beef Industry Council.

Granny Smith Pork

This apple-spiced dish is great served over rice.

6 Servings/Serving Size: 3 oz	
Exchanges:	
1 1/2	Fruit
3	Very Lean Meat
1	Fat
Calories	244
Calories from Fat	50
Total Fat	6 g
Saturated Fat	2 g
Cholesterol	56 mg
Sodium	135 mg
Carbohydrate	26 g
Dietary Fiber	3 g
Sugars	18 g
Protein	20 g

1 tsp canola oil
1 1/2 lb boneless pork, cut into
    1/2-inch cubes
4 medium Granny Smith apples, cored and
    sliced into 1/2-inch wedges
1 cup dry white wine
2 Tbsp brown sugar
1/4 cup cider vinegar
3 Tbsp cornstarch or arrowroot powder
2 Tbsp Worcestershire sauce
Fresh ground pepper and salt to taste

1. Heat the oil in a skillet over medium-high heat. Add the pork and brown on all sides. Add the apple slices and saute for 3 minutes. Add 1/2 cup of the wine, reduce the heat, cover, and simmer for 10 minutes.
2. Mix the other 1/2 cup of wine together with the remaining ingredients and add to the skillet. Cook over medium heat, stirring constantly, until sauce thickens.

Preparation time: 15 minutes

This adapted recipe is courtesy of the National Pork Producers.

Great Grains Burger

This is a delicious, no-meat, burger alternative.

6 Servings/Serving Size: 3–4 oz	
Exchanges:	
2	Starch
1/2 Monounsaturated Fat	

Calories	171
Calories from Fat	43
Total Fat	5 g
Saturated Fat	1 g
Cholesterol	37 mg
Sodium	72 mg
Carbohydrate	27 g
Dietary Fiber	3 g
Sugars	2 g
Protein	5 g

Preparation time: 20 minutes

1 Tbsp olive oil
1/2 cup minced mushrooms
1 small onion, minced
1/4 cup ground oats
3 cups cooked short-grain brown rice (this rice is stickier, so the burger holds together better on the grill)
1 egg, beaten
2 Tbsp Parmesan cheese
1 Tbsp Worcestershire sauce

1. Heat the oil in a small skillet over medium-high heat. Add the mushrooms and onions and saute until the mushrooms are dark and the onion is golden, about 6–7 minutes.
2. Prepare an outside grill with an oiled rack set 6 inches above the heat source. On a gas grill, set the heat to medium.
3. Combine the mushrooms and onions with the remaining ingredients. Form the mixture into 6 patties. Grill the burgers, turning once, for a total of 6–7 minutes until the outside is golden brown.

Grilled Filet au Poivre

Try these tender filets on a special occasion.

6 Servings/Serving Size: 3–4 oz
Exchanges: 3   Lean Meat

Calories 166
  Calories from Fat . . 91
Total Fat . . . . 10 g
  Saturated Fat . . . . 3 g

Cholesterol . . . . 55 mg
Sodium. . . . . . 428 mg
Carbohydrate. . . . . 0 g
  Dietary Fiber. . . . . 0 g
  Sugars . . . . 0 g

Protein . . . . 18 g

4 5-oz filet mignon steaks
2 tsp olive oil
5 Tbsp coarsely cracked black peppercorns
1 tsp salt

1. Rub each filet with some of the olive oil. Place the peppercorns on a piece of waxed paper. Press the steaks into the peppercorns to coat.
2. Prepare an outside grill with an oiled rack set 6 inches above the heat source. On a gas grill, set the heat to medium. Grill the filets, turning once, according to the following guidelines: 10–12 minutes for rare, 12–15 minutes for medium, or 17–18 minutes for well done.
3. Sprinkle the steaks with salt and serve.

Preparation time: 10 minutes

Grilled Ham Steak with Apricot Glaze

Just a few ingredients turn ham into something special!
(This recipe is high in sodium.)

6 Servings/Serving Size: 3 oz	
Exchanges:	
1/2	Fruit
3	Very Lean Meat
1/2	Fat
Calories 160	
Calories from Fat . . 46	
Total Fat . . . . 5 g	
Saturated Fat . . . . 2 g	
Cholesterol . . . . 50 mg	
Sodium . . . . . 1224 mg	
Carbohydrate . . . . . 4 g	
Dietary Fiber . . . . . 0 g	
Sugars . . . . 4 g	
Protein . . . . 23 g	

1/4 cup low-sugar apricot jam
2 tsp Dijon mustard
2 tsp cider vinegar
1 1/2 lb boneless, lean ham, cut into
6 1/2-inch-thick slices

In a small bowl, mix together the jam, mustard, and vinegar. Broil or grill the ham slices, brushing with the basting sauce and turning once, for 8–10 minutes.

Preparation time: 10 minutes

This adapted recipe is courtesy of the National Pork Producers.

Ham with Blueberry Sauce

Juicy, plump blueberries form the basis of this delicious sauce. (This recipe is high in sodium.)

6 Servings/Serving Size: 3 oz

Exchanges:

1	Fruit
4	Very Lean Meat
1/2	Fat

Calories	224
Calories from Fat	56
Total Fat	6 g
Saturated Fat	2 g

Cholesterol	60 mg
Sodium	1463 mg
Carbohydrate	12 g
Dietary Fiber	1 g
Sugars	9 g

Protein	27 g

1 2-lb, fully cooked, center slice of ham, cut 1 inch thick
1/3 cup water
1 Tbsp cornstarch or arrowroot powder
1/3 cup low-sugar apricot jam
1 Tbsp brown sugar
2 Tbsp dry red wine
4 tsp lemon juice
1 cup blueberries

1. Preheat the oven to 350 degrees. Trim the fat from the edge of the ham slice, if necessary. Place the ham slice on a rack in a shallow baking pan and bake for 30 minutes.
2. In a small saucepan, combine the cornstarch or arrowroot powder and water. Stir in the apricot jam, brown sugar, wine, and lemon juice. Cook over medium-low heat for 5–6 minutes until the sauce is thickened and bubbly. Stir in the blueberries and cook 2–3 minutes. Spoon the sauce over the ham and serve.

Preparation time: 15 minutes

This adapted recipe is courtesy of the National Pork Producers.

Honey-Mustard Lamb Chops

Mustard and honey gently flavor these lamb chops.

6 Servings/Serving Size: 2–3 oz	
Exchanges:	
1/2	Carbohydrate
2	Lean Meat
Calories 139	
Calories from Fat . . 54	
Total Fat . . . . 6 g	
Saturated Fat . . . . 2 g	
Cholesterol . . . . 52 mg	
Sodium . . . . . . 45 mg	
Carbohydrate . . . . . 5 g	
Dietary Fiber . . . . . 0 g	
Sugars . . . . 5 g	
Protein . . . . 16 g	

2 Tbsp honey
2 Tbsp fresh lemon juice
2 Tbsp minced fresh rosemary
1/2 tsp Dijon mustard
1 tsp minced garlic
1 tsp onion powder
1/2 tsp dry mustard
6 5-oz lamb chops, trimmed of fat
6 sprigs fresh mint

1. Combine all ingredients except the lamb chops and mint in a small bowl and microwave for 1 minute.
2. Brush the mixture on the chops and broil or grill, turning frequently, according to the following guidelines: 12 minutes for rare, 15 minutes for medium, and 18 minutes for well done. Garnish with mint and serve.

Preparation time: 10 minutes

Honey-Mustard Steak

The tang of spicy brown mustard and the sweetness of apple juice make this steak a stand-out.

6 Servings/Serving Size: 3–4 oz

Exchanges:
3   Lean Meat

Calories 158
  Calories from Fat . . 51
Total Fat . . . . 6 g
  Saturated Fat . . . . 2 g

Cholesterol . . . . 65 mg
Sodium . . . . . 300 mg
Carbohydrate . . . . . 2 g
  Dietary Fiber . . . . . 0 g
  Sugars . . . . 2 g

Protein . . . . 23 g

1/2 cup spicy brown mustard
2 Tbsp apple juice concentrate
1 tsp cinnamon
1 Tbsp honey
1 1/2 lb boneless top sirloin steak, well
  trimmed

1. Prepare an outside grill with an oiled rack set 6 inches above the heat source. On a gas grill, set the heat to medium.
2. Mix the mustard sauce ingredients together and brush one side of the steak with the sauce.
3. Grill the steak, turning once and brushing with more sauce, according to the following guidelines: 14 minutes for rare, 20 minutes for medium, or 26 minutes for well done. Carve into thin slices to serve.

Preparation time: 5 minutes

Indian Kabobs

Serve these kabobs with saffron rice and crisp cucumbers for a royal meal.

6 Servings/Serving Size: 1 kabob	
Exchanges:	
1/2	Fruit
1	Vegetable
3	Lean Meat
Calories 231	
Calories from Fat . . 72	
Total Fat . . . . 8 g	
Saturated Fat . . . . 3 g	
Cholesterol . . . 111 mg	
Sodium. . . . . . 194 mg	
Carbohydrate. . . . 11 g	
Dietary Fiber. . . . . 1 g	
Sugars . . . . 8 g	
Protein . . . . 28 g	

1/2 cup low-fat cottage cheese
1 1/2 lb ground lamb
1 medium onion, minced
1/3 cup raisins
1 Tbsp curry powder
1 egg
2 tsp minced fresh parsley
2 tsp cumin
Fresh ground pepper and salt to taste
18 cherry tomatoes

1. Soak 6 wooden skewers in water for 15 minutes. Blend the cottage cheese in a blender until smooth. Add the remaining ingredients except the cherry tomatoes. Mix until blended and then form the mixture into 24 meatballs.
2. Starting and ending with a meatball, alternately thread the meatballs and cherry tomatoes onto 6 wooden skewers. Oven broil the kabobs for about 10–15 minutes until the lamb is cooked through.

Preparation time: 20 minutes

Lamb and Asparagus Dinner

Set some daffodils on your table to complement this spring meal!

6 Servings/Serving Size:
3 oz lamb with
1/2 cup asparagus

Exchanges:	
2	Vegetable
3	Lean Meat

Calories 205	
Calories from Fat . . 64	
Total Fat . . . . 7 g	
Saturated Fat . . . . 2 g	

Cholesterol . . . . 75 mg	
Sodium. . . . . . 112 mg	
Carbohydrate. . . . . 8 g	
Dietary Fiber. . . . . 2 g	
Sugars . . . . 4 g	

Protein . . . . 26 g	

1/2 cup dry white wine
3 garlic cloves, minced
1 cup chopped red onion
1 1/2 lb boneless lamb, cut into cubes
3 cups lightly steamed, sliced, fresh
   asparagus
Fresh ground pepper and salt to taste

1. In a medium skillet over medium-high heat, add half the wine. Bring to a boil and add the garlic and onion. Saute for 5 minutes.
2. Add the lamb and saute for 6 more minutes. Add the remaining wine and asparagus. Cook, covered, for 5–8 minutes until lamb is tender. Add pepper and salt to taste.

Preparation time: 25 minutes

Mexican Burgers

Crushed tortilla chips give this burger a great texture and an interesting bite!

6 Servings/Serving Size: 3–4 oz

Exchanges:
4   Very Lean Meat

Calories	136
Calories from Fat	7
Total Fat	1 g
Saturated Fat	0 g
Cholesterol	75 mg
Sodium	78 mg
Carbohydrate	3 g
Dietary Fiber	1 g
Sugars	0 g
Protein	28 g

1 1/2 lb ground turkey (have your butcher grind this for you)
2 Tbsp ice water
2 Tbsp hot salsa
1/4 cup finely crushed, low-fat tortilla chips
2 tsp ground cumin
1/2 tsp chili powder

1. Prepare an outside grill with an oiled rack set 4 inches above the heat source. On a gas grill, set the heat to high.
2. Combine the meat with the remaining ingredients. Shape into 6 patties. Grill the burgers, turning once, for a total of 8–10 minutes until the turkey is white throughout.

Preparation time: 10 minutes

Mexican Roll-Ups

These roll-up sandwiches are easy to make and fun to eat!

6 Servings/Serving Size:
3 oz roast beef in a
12-inch tortilla

Exchanges:

2	Starch
1	Vegetable
4	Lean Meat
1/2	Monounsaturated Fat

Calories	426
Calories from Fat	147
Total Fat	16 g
Saturated Fat	4 g
Cholesterol	86 mg
Sodium	475 mg
Carbohydrate	34 g
Dietary Fiber	2 g
Sugars	3 g
Protein	33 g

6 12-inch whole-wheat flour tortillas
6 large romaine lettuce leaves
1 1/4 lb thinly sliced cooked roast beef
1 cup diced tomatoes
1 cup diced red and yellow peppers
2 Tbsp olive oil
3 Tbsp red wine vinegar
2 tsp cumin

1. For each roll-up, tear off about a 15-inch piece of either waxed paper or aluminum foil. Place the tortilla flat on the paper or foil. Place a romaine lettuce leaf on top of the tortilla. Add 3 oz beef on top of the lettuce. Divide the tomatoes, peppers, oil, vinegar, and cumin over the beef for each roll-up.

2. Begin rolling the paper or foil over the tortilla to encase the filling. Roll until the sandwich is completely rolled up. Fold the excess paper or foil over the top and bottom of the roll-up. To eat, peel back the paper or foil.

Preparation time: 15 minutes

Stuff-A-Burger

A surprise awaits you in the center of a juicy burger.

6 Servings/Serving Size: 3–4 oz	
Exchanges:	
4	Very Lean Meat
1/2	Fat
Calories 163	
Calories from Fat . . 50	
Total Fat . . . . 6.5 g	
Saturated Fat . . . . 2 g	
Cholesterol . . . . 65 mg	
Sodium . . . . . . 175 mg	
Carbohydrate . . . . . 0 g	
Dietary Fiber . . . . . 0 g	
Sugars . . . . 1 g	
Protein . . . . 28 g	

1 1/2 lb lean ground sirloin
2 Tbsp ice water
Fresh ground pepper and salt to taste

Choose from the following stuffings
(use 1 Tbsp or a combination equal to
1 Tbsp per burger):
　　Hot salsa
　　Parmesan cheese
　　Chili sauce
　　Minced jalapeno peppers
　　Bleu cheese
　　Teriyaki sauce
　　Marinara sauce
　　Minced sauteed mushrooms
　　Hoisin sauce
　　Minced smoked ham
　　Minced roasted red pepper
　　Feta cheese

Preparation time: 10 minutes

1. Mix together the ground sirloin with
   the water, pepper, and salt. Form into
   12 small patties. Place 1 Tbsp of desired
   filling in the center of each of 6 patties.
   Top each patty with one of the remaining
   patties. Seal edges to secure filling inside.
2. Prepare an outdoor grill with an oiled
   rack set 4 inches above the coals. On a
   gas grill, set heat to high.
3. Grill the burgers on both sides according
   to the following guidelines: 5–6 minutes
   for rare, 7–9 minutes for medium, or
   10–12 minutes for well done.

Tenderloin Kabobs with Rosemary

Use rosemary stems as brushes to baste these kabobs with port wine and olive oil.

6 Servings/Serving Size: 3–4 oz beef plus vegetables

Exchanges:

| 1 | Vegetable |
| 3 | Medium-Fat Meat |

Calories	255
Calories from Fat .	126
Total Fat	14 g
Saturated Fat	4 g
Cholesterol	66 mg
Sodium	55 mg
Carbohydrate.	7 g
Dietary Fiber.	2 g
Sugars	3 g
Protein	23 g

Preparation time: 20 minutes

1 1/2 lb beef tenderloin, cut into 1-inch cubes
12 large mushroom caps (remove stems from mushrooms)
1 medium red pepper, cut into 1-inch pieces
1 medium green pepper, cut into 1-inch pieces
12 cherry tomatoes
1 cup port wine
2 Tbsp olive oil
3 garlic cloves, finely minced
2 tsp minced fresh thyme
3 or 4 long, fresh rosemary stems

1. If using wooden kabob skewers, soak 6 of them in warm water for 15 minutes. This prevents the skewers from catching on fire while the kabobs cook. Then thread the beef, mushrooms, peppers, and cherry tomatoes on the skewers.
2. Combine the next four ingredients in a small saucepan and heat until the wine simmers. Keep on low heat. Dip the rosemary stems into the basting sauce and brush on the kabobs.
3. Prepare an outside grill with an oiled rack set 4 inches above the heat source. On a gas grill, set the heat to high.
4. Grill, turning constantly, for about 8–10 minutes total, until the meat is done as desired. Let everyone baste their own kabobs with a rosemary stem for grilling fun!

Tex-Mex Pork Chops

This is a quick, one-skillet dish with an olé touch!

6 Servings/Serving Size: 3 oz	
Exchanges:	
3	Lean Meat
Calories	168
Calories from Fat	70
Total Fat	8 g
Saturated Fat	2 g
Cholesterol	52 mg
Sodium	279 mg
Carbohydrate	4 g
Dietary Fiber	1 g
Sugars	2 g
Protein	19 g

2 tsp olive oil
6 4–5-oz boneless pork loin chops
1 1/2 cups salsa
1 4-oz can diced green chilies
1/2 tsp ground cumin

Heat the oil in a skillet over medium-high heat. Add the pork chops and saute for about 3 minutes on each side. Add the remaining ingredients. Lower the heat, cover, and simmer for 10 minutes.

Preparation time: 15 minutes

Grilled Meats

(these recipes require marinating for several hours or overnight before a quick cooking time of 15–20 minutes)

Caribbean Pork Kabobs

These kabobs go very well with grilled fruit.

6 Servings/Serving Size: 3–4 oz	
Exchanges:	
4	Very Lean Meat
Calories	147
Calories from Fat	37
Total Fat	4 g
Saturated Fat	1 g
Cholesterol	66 mg
Sodium	48 mg
Carbohydrate	2 g
Dietary Fiber	0 g
Sugars	2 g
Protein	24 g

1 1/2 lb pork tenderloin, cut into
   1-inch cubes
1/2 cup orange juice
1/4 cup lime juice
2 tsp brown sugar
1/2 tsp minced fresh thyme
1/2 tsp ground nutmeg
1/4 tsp ground cloves
1/4 tsp cayenne pepper

1. Combine all ingredients and place in a plastic bag. Let the pork cubes marinate in the refrigerator for at least 2 hours or up to 24 hours. If using wooden kabob skewers, soak 6 of them in warm water for 15 minutes. This prevents the skewers from catching on fire while the kabobs cook.
2. Prepare an outside grill with an oiled rack set 4 inches above the heat source. On a gas grill, set the heat to high. Remove the cubes from the bag and thread them on the skewers. Grill the kabobs for 12–15 minutes total until the pork is cooked through.

Preparation time: 10 minutes

This adapted recipe is courtesy of the National Pork Producers.

Cathy's Marinated Chicken

This simple chicken is great served with rice pilaf and a crisp salad.

6 Servings/Serving Size:
3–4 oz

Exchanges:
4   Very Lean Meat
1/2 Monounsaturated Fat

Calories	175
Calories from Fat	48
Total Fat	5 g
Saturated Fat	1 g
Cholesterol	73 mg
Sodium	270 mg
Carbohydrate	2 g
Dietary Fiber	0 g
Sugars	1 g
Protein	27 g

1 cup dry white wine
1 cup fresh lemon juice
2 Tbsp olive oil
1/4 cup lite soy sauce
1 1/2 lb boneless, skinless chicken breast

1. Mix the marinade ingredients together and pour over the chicken. Marinate in the refrigerator overnight.
2. Grill or broil the chicken 6 inches from the heat source on each side for 5–8 minutes until juices run clear.

Preparation time: 5 minutes

Chicken in Fragrant Spices

Using a technique called scoring helps ensure that a marinade penetrates deep into the potentially tough chicken fibers.

6 Servings/Serving Size: 3–4 oz	

Exchanges:	
4	Very Lean Meat

Calories 140	
Calories from Fat . . 26	
Total Fat . . . . 3 g	
Saturated Fat . . . . 1 g	

Cholesterol . . . . 69 mg	
Sodium . . . . . . 66 mg	
Carbohydrate. . . . . 1 g	
Dietary Fiber. . . . . 0 g	
Sugars . . . . 1 g	

Protein . . . . 26 g	

1 1/2 lb boneless, skinless chicken breasts
3 garlic cloves, minced
2 Tbsp minced ginger
1 Tbsp cumin
1/2 tsp turmeric
1/4 cup plain nonfat yogurt, stirred until smooth

1. Make three diagonal slashes in the flesh of each chicken breast. Combine all remaining ingredients. Add the chicken breasts and coat well with the mixture. Marinate at least 8 hours or up to 48 hours.
2. Prepare an outside grill with an oiled rack set 4 inches above the heat source. On a gas grill, set the heat to high. Grill the chicken breasts for 3–4 minutes on each side until the chicken is cooked through.

Preparation time: 10 minutes

Chicken Satay

A satay is a spicy Indian kabob.

6 Servings/Serving Size: 3–4 oz

Exchanges:

4	Very Lean Meat
1/2	Fat

Calories	162
Calories from Fat	43
Total Fat	5 g
Saturated Fat	1 g
Cholesterol	69 mg
Sodium	60 mg
Carbohydrate	3 g
Dietary Fiber	0 g
Sugars	3 g
Protein	25 g

1 Tbsp corn oil
3 Tbsp lime juice
3 garlic cloves
1 red chili, minced
1 Tbsp honey
1 tsp ground coriander seeds
1 1/2 lb boneless, skinless chicken breasts, cubed into 1-inch pieces

1. In a blender, combine all ingredients for the satay sauce. Place the chicken cubes in a bowl, cover with the sauce, and marinate in the refrigerator for 4 hours. Prepare an outside grill with an oiled rack set 4 inches above the heat source. On a gas grill, set the heat to high.
2. If using wooden kabob skewers, soak 6 of them in warm water for 15 minutes. This prevents the skewers from catching on fire while the kabobs cook. Then thread the chicken cubes on the skewers. Grill the satays for about 4–5 minutes total, until the chicken is cooked through.

Preparation time: 15 minutes

Grilled Caribbean Chicken Breasts

Imagine tropical breezes and an ocean sunset accompanying this Caribbean chicken.

6 Servings/Serving Size: 3–4 oz	
Exchanges: 4 Very Lean Meat	
Calories 154	
Calories from Fat . . 41	
Total Fat . . . . 5 g	
Saturated Fat . . . . 1 g	
Cholesterol . . . . 69 mg	
Sodium . . . . . . 61 mg	
Carbohydrate. . . . . 1 g	
Dietary Fiber. . . . . 0 g	
Sugars . . . . 1 g	
Protein . . . . 25 g	

1/4 cup fresh squeezed orange juice
1 tsp orange peel
1 Tbsp olive oil
1 Tbsp lime juice
1 tsp minced ginger
2 garlic cloves, minced
1/4 tsp hot pepper sauce
1/2 tsp minced fresh oregano
1 1/2 lb boneless, skinless chicken breasts, halved

1. In a blender, combine all ingredients except the chicken. Pour the marinade over the chicken breasts and marinate in the refrigerator at least 2 hours or up to 48 hours.
2. Grill or broil the chicken for about 6 minutes per side until no trace of pink remains.

Preparation time: 10 minutes

This adapted recipe is courtesy of the National Broiler Council.

Grilled Chicken with Herbs

This chicken is also delicious served cold the next day.

6 Servings/Serving Size: 3–4 oz

Exchanges:
4   Very Lean Meat
1 Monounsaturated Fat

Calories 197
  Calories from Fat . . 87
Total Fat . . . . 10 g
  Saturated Fat . . . . 2 g

Cholesterol . . . . 69 mg
Sodium . . . . . . 78 mg
Carbohydrate . . . . . 1 g
  Dietary Fiber . . . . . 0 g
  Sugars . . . . 1 g

Protein . . . . 25 g

2 Tbsp minced fresh Italian parsley
2 tsp minced fresh rosemary
2 tsp minced fresh thyme
1 sage leaf
3 garlic cloves, minced
1/4 cup olive oil
1/2 cup balsamic vinegar
Fresh ground pepper and salt to taste
1 1/2 lb boneless, skinless chicken breasts, halved

1. In a blender, combine all ingredients except the chicken. Pour the marinade over the chicken breasts and marinate in the refrigerator at least 2 hours or up to 48 hours.
2. Grill or broil the chicken for about 6 minutes per side until no trace of pink remains.

Preparation time: 10 minutes

Grilled Cornish Game Hens

Soy sauce gives these hens a delicate Asian flavor.

6 Servings/Serving Size: 1/2 hen without skin	
Exchanges:	
2	Very Lean Meat
Calories 64	
Calories from Fat . . 16	
Total Fat . . . . 2 g	
Saturated Fat . . . . 0 g	
Cholesterol . . . . 47 mg	
Sodium . . . . . . 78 mg	
Carbohydrate . . . . . 1 g	
Dietary Fiber . . . . . 0 g	
Sugars . . . . 1 g	
Protein . . . . 10 g	

3 Cornish game hens, split in half
3 garlic cloves
2 small shallots
2 tsp sugar
1 tsp cinnamon
2 Tbsp lite soy sauce
2 Tbsp dry sherry

1. Prepare the hens by washing them inside and out and discarding the giblets. With poultry shears, cut each hen in half. In a food processor, grind together the garlic, shallots, sugar, and cinnamon until the mixture is paste-like. Place in a bowl and stir in the soy sauce and sherry.
2. Rub the marinade over the Cornish hens and let them marinate in the refrigerator at least 2 hours or up to 48 hours. Then, prepare an outside grill with an oiled rack set 4 inches from the heat source. On a gas grill, set the heat to high. Grill the hens for 30 minutes, turning once, until juices run clear.

Preparation time: 15 minutes

Grilled Pepper Pork

To make this dish more spicy, try using white Szechwan peppercorns, available in Asian grocery stores.

6 Servings/Serving Size: 3 oz	
Exchanges:	
3	Lean Meat
Calories	140
Calories from Fat	55
Total Fat	6 g
Saturated Fat	2 g
Cholesterol	52 mg
Sodium	189 mg
Carbohydrate	1 g
Dietary Fiber	0 g
Sugars	1 g
Protein	19 g

2 garlic cloves, crushed
1 Tbsp crushed coriander seeds
8 crushed black or white peppercorns
1 tsp brown sugar
3 Tbsp lite soy sauce
6 4–5-oz pork loin chops, about 1 inch thick

Combine all ingredients except the pork chops, then add the chops and marinate for 30 minutes. Grill or broil the chops, brushing with marinade and turning once, for about 12–14 minutes.

Preparation time: 15 minutes

This adapted recipe is courtesy of the National Pork Producers.

Herbed Chuck Steaks

Red wine vinegar acts as the perfect tenderizer for beef chuck steaks.

6 Servings/Serving Size: 3–4 oz	
Exchanges:	
4	Lean Meat
Calories 225	
Calories from Fat . . 89	
Total Fat . . . . 10 g	
Saturated Fat . . . . 3 g	
Cholesterol . . . . 94 mg	
Sodium . . . . . . 86 mg	
Carbohydrate. . . . . 1 g	
Dietary Fiber. . . . . 0 g	
Sugars . . . . 1 g	
Protein . . . . 31 g	

1/3 cup red wine vinegar
1/3 cup water
1 Tbsp olive oil
1 Tbsp minced fresh thyme
1/2 tsp sugar
Fresh ground pepper and salt to taste
2 lb boneless beef chuck steak, well trimmed

1. Combine all marinade ingredients, then add the chuck steak and marinate in the refrigerator for 6–8 hours. Prepare an outside grill with an oiled rack set 6 inches above the heat source. On a gas grill, set the heat to medium. Remove the steak from the marinade and reserve the marinade.
2. Grill the steak, turning once and brushing with reserved marinade, according to the following guidelines: 14 minutes for rare, 20 minutes for medium, or 26 minutes for well done. Carve into thin slices to serve.

Preparation time: 10 minutes

This adapted recipe is courtesy of the Beef Board and Veal Committee/ Beef Industry Council.

Lemon-Lime Chicken

This is a great dish to serve for a light spring luncheon.

6 Servings/Serving Size: 3–4 oz
Exchanges:
4   Very Lean Meat
1/2 Monounsaturated Fat
Calories 157
Calories from Fat . . 47
Total Fat . . . . 5 g
Saturated Fat . . . . 1 g
Cholesterol . . . . 69 mg
Sodium . . . . . . 74 mg
Carbohydrate. . . . . 1 g
Dietary Fiber. . . . . 0 g
Sugars . . . . 1 g
Protein . . . . 25 g

2 Tbsp fresh lemon juice
2 Tbsp fresh lime juice
2 Tbsp olive oil
2 tsp sugar
2 tsp minced fresh thyme
1/4 cup low-fat, low-sodium chicken broth
Fresh ground pepper and salt to taste
1 1/2 lb chicken breasts, boned, skinned, and halved

1. In a blender, combine all ingredients except the chicken. Pour the marinade over the chicken breasts and marinate in the refrigerator at least 2 hours or up to 48 hours.
2. Grill or broil the chicken for about 6 minutes per side until no trace of pink remains.

Preparation time: 15 minutes

Mango-Lime Chicken

You can almost feel the tropical breezes when you taste this fruity chicken.

6 Servings/Serving Size: 3–4 oz	

Exchanges:
4	Very Lean Meat
1/2	Monounsaturated Fat

Calories	162
Calories from Fat	38
Total Fat	4 g
Saturated Fat	1 g
Cholesterol	73 mg
Sodium	71 mg
Carbohydrate	3 g
Dietary Fiber	0 g
Sugars	2 g
Protein	27 g

3 chicken breasts, boned, halved, and skinned
1/4 cup orange juice
2 Tbsp fresh lime juice
2 Tbsp mango chutney
2 tsp grated fresh ginger
1 Tbsp olive oil
1/2 tsp hot pepper sauce
1 tsp minced fresh oregano
2 garlic cloves, minced

1. Combine the chicken breasts with all remaining ingredients. Place in the refrigerator and marinate overnight.
2. The next day, prepare an outside grill with an oiled rack set 6 inches above the heat source. On a gas grill, set the heat to medium. Grill the chicken breasts for 6 minutes on each side until the chicken is cooked through.

Preparation time: 10 minutes

Marinated Lamb Chops

Red wine and raspberry vinegar add a fruity flavor to traditional lamb chops.

6 Servings/Serving Size: 3 oz	
Exchanges:	
2	Lean Meat
1/2	Fat
Calories 135	
Calories from Fat . . 58	
Total Fat . . . . 6 g	
Saturated Fat . . . . 2 g	
Cholesterol . . . . 56 mg	
Sodium . . . . . . 86 mg	
Carbohydrate. . . . . 1 g	
Dietary Fiber. . . . . 0 g	
Sugars . . . . 1 g	
Protein . . . . 17 g	

1/2 cup dry red wine
1/4 cup raspberry vinegar
2 Tbsp Dijon mustard
Fresh ground pepper and salt to taste
2 lb lamb chops

Combine the first four ingredients. Add the lamb chops and marinate in the refrigerator for 1–2 hours. Grill or broil the lamb chops until done as desired.

Preparation time: 10 minutes

Mediterranean Grilled Lamb

Use bread or pasta to soak up the juices from this delicious dish.

6 Servings/Serving Size: 3 oz	
Exchanges:	
3 . . . . Lean Meat	
Calories 158	
Calories from Fat . . 77	
Total Fat . . . . 9 g	
Saturated Fat . . . . 3 g	
Cholesterol . . . . 62 mg	
Sodium . . . . . . 70 mg	
Carbohydrate . . . . . 1 g	
Dietary Fiber . . . . . 0 g	
Sugars . . . . 1 g	
Protein . . . . 19 g	

1/3 cup minced red onion
2 Tbsp olive oil
1/4 cup balsamic vinegar
3 garlic cloves, minced
1 Tbsp minced fresh basil
Fresh ground pepper and salt to taste
6 4–5-oz lamb chops

Combine all ingredients except the lamb chops, then add the lamb chops and marinate in the refrigerator at least 3–5 hours. Grill or broil the lamb chops until done as desired.

Preparation time: 15 minutes

Mustard and Sesame Chicken

Dijon mustard adds a twist to this soy-based marinade.

6 Servings/Serving Size: 3–4 oz	
Exchanges:	
4	Very Lean Meat
Calories 160	
Calories from Fat . . 35	
Total Fat . . . . 4 g	
Saturated Fat . . . . 1 g	
Cholesterol . . . . 69 mg	
Sodium. . . . . . 581 mg	
Carbohydrate. . . . . 4 g	
Dietary Fiber. . . . . 0 g	
Sugars . . . . 3 g	
Protein . . . . 26 g	

2 scallions, minced
3 garlic cloves, minced
2 shallots, minced
1/2 cup lite soy sauce
2 Tbsp Dijon mustard
1 Tbsp oyster sauce
1 Tbsp Hoisin sauce
2 tsp hot pepper sauce
1 cup low-fat, low-sodium chicken broth
2 tsp sesame oil
2 tsp honey
1 1/2 lb boneless, skinless chicken breasts, halved

1. In a blender, combine all ingredients except the chicken. Pour the marinade over the chicken breasts and marinate in the refrigerator at least 2 hours or up to 48 hours.
2. Grill or broil the chicken for about 6 minutes per side until no trace of pink remains.

Preparation time: 10 minutes

Old-Fashioned Barbecued Sirloin

Instead of slapping on commercial barbecue sauce, let this sirloin marinate overnight for an authentic smoky taste.

6 Servings/Serving Size: 3–4 oz	
Exchanges:	
4	Lean Meat
Calories 227	
Calories from Fat . . 91	
Total Fat . . . . 10 g	
Saturated Fat . . . . 3 g	
Cholesterol . . . . 87 mg	
Sodium . . . . . . 77 mg	
Carbohydrate. . . . . 3 g	
Dietary Fiber. . . . . 1 g	
Sugars . . . . 1 g	
Protein . . . . 30 g	

1 Tbsp chili powder
2 tsp minced ginger
2 garlic cloves, minced
1 small onion, minced
1/3 cup lemon juice
2 Tbsp olive oil
2 tsp paprika
2 lb boneless top sirloin steak, well trimmed

1. Combine all marinade ingredients, then add the sirloin and marinate in the refrigerator overnight. Prepare an outside grill with an oiled rack set 6 inches above the heat source. On a gas grill, set the heat to medium.
2. Grill the sirloin, turning once, according to the following guidelines: 15–20 minutes for rare, 25–30 minutes for medium, or 35–40 minutes for well done. Carve into thin slices to serve.

Preparation time: 10 minutes

Raspberry Chicken

Using raspberry vinegar with chicken is a great way to add a burst of flavor.

6 Servings/Serving Size: 3–4 oz	

Exchanges:
4   Very Lean Meat

Calories 155
 Calories from Fat . . 36
Total Fat . . . . 4 g
 Saturated Fat . . . . 1 g

Cholesterol . . . . 69 mg
Sodium . . . . . . 72 mg
Carbohydrate . . . . . 3 g
 Dietary Fiber . . . . . 0 g
 Sugars . . . . 3 g

Protein . . . . 25 g

3 Tbsp water
1/2 cup raspberry vinegar
1 Tbsp olive oil
2 Tbsp honey
1 tsp orange extract
1 tsp minced fresh rosemary
1/2 tsp nutmeg
Fresh ground pepper and salt to taste
1 1/2 lb boneless, skinless chicken breasts

1. Combine all ingredients except the chicken in a small bowl and microwave for 1 minute. Pour into a plastic bag. Add the chicken and marinate in the refrigerator at least 1 hour.
2. Prepare an outside grill with an oiled rack set 6 inches above the heat source. On a gas grill, set the heat to medium. Grill the chicken breasts for 6 minutes on each side until the chicken is cooked through.

Preparation time: 15 minutes

Simply Great Grilled Chicken

You'll never find more moist grilled chicken!

6 Servings/Serving Size: 3–4 oz	
Exchanges:	
4	Very Lean Meat
1/2	Fat
Calories 164	
Calories from Fat . . 42	
Total Fat . . . . 5 g	
Saturated Fat . . . . 1 g	
Cholesterol . . . . 69 mg	
Sodium. . . . . . 665 mg	
Carbohydrate. . . . . 2 g	
Dietary Fiber. . . . . 0 g	
Sugars . . . . 2 g	
Protein . . . . 25 g	

1/2 cup lite soy sauce
1/4 cup dry sherry
1 Tbsp canola oil
2 garlic cloves, minced
1 tsp minced ginger
1/4 tsp nutmeg
Fresh ground pepper to taste
1 1/2 lb boneless, skinless chicken breasts

1. Combine all marinade ingredients. Pour half the mixture over the chicken and set in the refrigerator to marinate for at least 2 hours or up to 24 hours. Save the remaining mixture for basting.
2. Prepare an outside grill with an oiled rack set 4 inches above the heat source. On a gas grill, set the heat to high. Grill the chicken breasts for 3–4 minutes on each side, turning once and basting with extra marinade, until the chicken is cooked through.

Preparation time: 10 minutes

This adapted recipe is courtesy of the National Broiler Council.

Spicy Indian Chicken

Serve tall goblets of cool water with this spicy dish!

6 Servings/Serving Size: 3–4 oz

Exchanges:

4   Very Lean Meat

Calories	143
Calories from Fat	26
Total Fat	3 g
Saturated Fat	1 g
Cholesterol	69 mg
Sodium	72 mg
Carbohydrate	2 g
Dietary Fiber	0 g
Sugars	1 g
Protein	26 g

1 1/2 cups plain nonfat yogurt
2 tsp cayenne pepper
2 small red chilies, minced
2 tsp minced ginger
1 tsp ground coriander
2 garlic cloves, minced
2 tsp cumin
2 tsp mustard seeds
1 tsp paprika
1/4 tsp allspice
1 1/2 lb boneless, skinless chicken breasts, halved

1. In a blender, combine all ingredients except the chicken. Pour the marinade over the chicken breasts and marinate in the refrigerator at least 2 hours or up to 48 hours.
2. Grill or broil the chicken for about 6 minutes per side until no trace of pink remains.

Preparation time: 10 minutes

Spicy Pita Pockets

Give your family something they can sink their teeth into!

6 Servings/Serving Size: 3–4 oz filling	
Exchanges:	
2	Starch
1	Vegetable
4	Lean Meat
1/2	Fat

Calories 422	
Calories from Fat . 148	
Total Fat . . . . 16 g	
Saturated Fat . . . . 8 g	
Cholesterol . . . . 90 mg	
Sodium. . . . . . 440 mg	
Carbohydrate. . . . 36 g	
Dietary Fiber. . . . . 3 g	
Sugars . . . . 5 g	
Protein . . . . 36 g	

1/2 cup fresh lime juice
2 Tbsp honey
2 Tbsp olive oil
2 garlic cloves, minced
1 tsp chili powder
1/2 tsp cumin
1 1/2 lb top sirloin steak, trimmed of all fat
6 large whole-wheat pita pockets
1 15-oz can Mexican-style chopped
   tomatoes, well drained
6 oz pepper jack cheese
12 romaine lettuce leaves

1. Combine the first six ingredients to make the marinade. Add the steak and marinate in the refrigerator for at least 6 hours. Then, prepare an outside grill with an oiled rack set 4 inches above the heat source. On a gas grill, set the heat to high.
2. Grill the steak until done as desired and cut into 24 thin slices. To assemble the sandwiches, open the pita bread to form a pocket. Add the steak to the pockets. Top with the tomatoes, cheese, and lettuce. Eat with a fork if necessary.

Preparation time: 10 minutes

Spicy Salsa Chicken Grill

Liven up your grilled chicken with the spice of salsa!

6 Servings/Serving Size: 3–4 oz	
Exchanges:	
4	Very Lean Meat
1/2	Monounsaturated Fat

Calories	158
Calories from Fat . .	47
Total Fat	5 g
Saturated Fat	1 g
Cholesterol	69 mg
Sodium	78 mg
Carbohydrate	1 g
Dietary Fiber	0 g
Sugars	1 g
Protein	25 g

1/3 cup fresh lime juice
2 tsp minced fresh chives
2 tsp minced ginger
2 garlic cloves, minced
2 Tbsp olive oil
2 tsp chili powder
1 cup hot salsa
1 1/2 lb boneless, skinless chicken breasts

1. In a small saucepan, mix together the lime juice, chives, ginger, and garlic. Add the olive oil and chili powder and heat to boiling over medium heat. Stir in the salsa. Allow sauce to cool. Place the chicken in a plastic bag. Add the sauce and let marinate in the refrigerator for at least 2 hours or up to 24 hours.
2. Prepare an outside grill with an oiled rack set 4 inches above the heat source. On a gas grill, set the heat to high. Grill the chicken breasts for 3–4 minutes on each side, turning once and basting with extra marinade, until the chicken is cooked through.

Preparation time: 15 minutes

This adapted recipe is courtesy of the National Broiler Council.

Tequila Turkey

Enjoy the flavors of this tipsy turkey.

6 Servings/Serving Size:
3–4 oz

Exchanges:
4   Very Lean Meat

Calories	151
Calories from Fat	26
Total Fat	3 g
Saturated Fat	1 g

Cholesterol	75 mg
Sodium	48 mg
Carbohydrate	1 g
Dietary Fiber	0 g
Sugars	1 g

Protein	27 g

1 1/2 lb turkey breast filets
1/2 cup lemon juice
2 Tbsp olive oil
1/4 cup tequila
2 garlic cloves, minced
1 small onion, thinly sliced
1/4 cup minced red pepper

1. Combine the turkey with the marinade ingredients. Marinate for at least 2 hours or up to 48 hours.
2. Prepare an outside grill with an oiled rack set 4 inches above the heat source. On a gas grill, set the heat to high. Grill the turkey for 3–4 minutes on each side until it is white throughout.

Preparation time: 10 minutes

Teriyaki Pineapple Chicken

Sweet pineapple rings top hot grilled chicken.

6 Servings/Serving Size: 3–4 oz

Exchanges:
4   Very Lean Meat

Calories	156
Calories from Fat	28
Total Fat	3 g
Saturated Fat	1 g
Cholesterol	73 mg
Sodium	309 mg
Carbohydrate	3 g
Dietary Fiber	0 g
Sugars	2 g
Protein	27 g

2 garlic cloves, minced
1/2 cup unsweetened pineapple juice
3 Tbsp Worcestershire sauce
1/4 cup teriyaki sauce
2 tsp hot pepper sauce
1 1/2 lb boneless, skinless chicken breasts

1. Combine all marinade ingredients in a plastic bag. Add the chicken breasts and marinate in the refrigerator at least 1 hour.
2. Prepare an outside grill with an oiled rack set 4 inches above the heat source. On a gas grill, set the heat to high. Grill the chicken breasts for 3–4 minutes on each side until the chicken is cooked through.

Preparation time: 5 minutes

Teriyaki Pork Chops

This easy marinade tenderizes the pork beautifully.

6 Servings/Serving Size: 3 oz	
Exchanges:	
3	Lean Meat
Calories 160	
Calories from Fat . . 65	
Total Fat . . . . 7 g	
Saturated Fat . . . . 2 g	
Cholesterol . . . . 52 mg	
Sodium. . . . . . 239 mg	
Carbohydrate. . . . . 3 g	
Dietary Fiber. . . . . 0 g	
Sugars . . . . 3 g	
Protein . . . . 19 g	

1/4 cup lite soy sauce
1/4 cup dry sherry
2 Tbsp sugar
3 garlic cloves, minced
1 Tbsp peanut oil
6 4–5-oz pork loin chops

Combine all marinade ingredients. Add the pork chops and marinate in the refrigerator for 4–24 hours. Grill or broil the pork chops, turning once, for 12–13 minutes until juices run clear.

Preparation time: 5 minutes

This adapted recipe is courtesy of the National Pork Producers.

Stir-Frys

Apple Turkey

Apple juice adds a sweet touch to this stir-fry.

6 Servings/Serving Size:
3–4 oz turkey with
1/2 cup rice

Exchanges:

2 1/2	Starch
1	Vegetable
3	Very Lean Meat

Calories	320
Calories from Fat	30
Total Fat	3 g
Saturated Fat	0 g

Cholesterol	75 mg
Sodium	285 mg
Carbohydrate	39 g
Dietary Fiber	3 g
Sugars	11 g

Protein	31 g

2 Tbsp brown sugar
1/2 tsp red pepper flakes
2 garlic cloves, minced
2 Tbsp dry sherry
2 Tbsp lite soy sauce
1 Tbsp cornstarch or arrowroot powder
1/2 cup unsweetened apple juice
1 1/2 lb turkey breast, cut into thin strips
1 Tbsp canola oil
1 cup fresh snow peas, trimmed
2 cups thinly sliced carrot
2 Tbsp sliced scallions
3 cups cooked rice

1. Combine the first seven ingredients. Add the turkey and mix to coat well. Let stand for 30 minutes. Heat the oil in a wok over high heat. Add the turkey mixture and stir-fry for 5–7 minutes.
2. Push the turkey up on the sides of the wok. Add the vegetables and stir-fry for 3 minutes. Push the turkey back to the center of the wok and stir-fry for 2–3 more minutes. Serve over hot rice.

Preparation time: 20 minutes

Asian Apple Pork

Asian spices and apples go well together.

6 Servings/Serving Size: 3 oz pork with 1/2 cup rice	
Exchanges:	
2	Starch
3	Very Lean Meat
1/2	Fat

Calories 285	
Calories from Fat . . 55	
Total Fat . . . . 6 g	
Saturated Fat . . . . 2 g	
Cholesterol . . . . 65 mg	
Sodium . . . . . . 268 mg	
Carbohydrate . . . . 30 g	
Dietary Fiber . . . . . 1 g	
Sugars . . . . 5 g	
Protein . . . . 26 g	

Preparation time: 10 minutes

2 tsp peanut oil
2 tsp minced ginger
2 Tbsp minced scallions
1 1/2 lb pork tenderloin, cut into 3-inch strips
1 cup diced Gala apples
2 Tbsp lite soy sauce
1 Tbsp rice vinegar
1 cup low-fat, low-sodium chicken broth
1 Tbsp brown sugar
2 tsp dry sherry
1 Tbsp cornstarch or arrowroot powder
2 Tbsp water
3 cups cooked jasmine, white, or brown rice

1. Heat the oil in a wok over high heat. Add the ginger and scallions and stir-fry for 30 seconds. Add the pork and stir-fry for 7–9 minutes until pork loses its pinkness. Add the apple and stir-fry for 3 more minutes.
2. Combine the soy sauce, vinegar, broth, brown sugar, and sherry. Add to the wok, lower heat, cover, and simmer for 5 minutes. Combine the cornstarch or arrowroot powder and water. Add to the wok and cook until thickened, about 3 minutes. Serve over cooked rice.

Gingered Tuna

Shredded cabbage, instead of rice or noodles, adds bulk to this stir-fry.

6 Servings/Serving Size:
3–4 oz tuna

Exchanges:
1	Vegetable
4	Very Lean Meat
1	Fat

Calories 218
Calories from Fat . . 71
Total Fat . . . . 8 g
Saturated Fat . . . . 2 g

Cholesterol . . . . 42 mg
Sodium . . . . . . 279 mg
Carbohydrate . . . . . 7 g
Dietary Fiber . . . . . 2 g
Sugars . . . . 4 g

Protein . . . . 27 g

1/2 cup dry sherry
3/4 cup orange juice
1/2 cup low-fat, low-sodium chicken broth
1/4 cup lite soy sauce
2 Tbsp minced ginger
1 1/2 lb tuna steaks, cut into 2-inch cubes
1 Tbsp sesame oil
1/2 cup chopped shallots
1 cup thinly sliced carrots
1/2 cup thinly sliced celery
1 cup shredded cabbage

1. Combine the first five ingredients. Add tuna and marinate for 30 minutes. Heat the oil in a wok over high heat. Add the shallots and stir-fry for 2 minutes. Add the carrots and celery and stir-fry for 3 minutes. Add the cabbage and stir-fry for 3 minutes.
2. Push the vegetables up on the sides of the wok. Remove the tuna from the marinade and add it to the wok. Stir-fry for 3–4 minutes. Add the vegetables back to the center of the wok and stir-fry for 2 more minutes.

Preparation time: 20 minutes

Holiday Shrimp

Jumbo shrimp are spiced up with this Chinese ginger sauce.

6 Servings/Serving Size:
3–4 oz with
1/2 cup rice

Exchanges:

2	Starch
2	Very Lean Meat

Calories 214
  Calories from Fat . . 26
Total Fat . . . . 3 g
  Saturated Fat . . . . 1 g

Cholesterol . . . 161 mg
Sodium. . . . . . 508 mg
Carbohydrate. . . . 26 g
  Dietary Fiber. . . . . 2 g
  Sugars . . . . 2 g

Protein . . . . 21 g

1 1/2 lb fresh jumbo shrimp, peeled,
    deveined, and butterflied (you can have
    the seafood department do this for you)
1 tsp corn oil
2 scallions, minced
2 tsp minced ginger
2 garlic cloves, minced
3/4 cup low-fat, low-sodium chicken broth
3 Tbsp lite soy sauce
2 Tbsp cider vinegar
2 tsp rice vinegar
1/4 tsp chili powder
1 Tbsp cornstarch or arrowroot powder
2 Tbsp water
3 cups cooked brown rice

1. Heat the oil in a large skillet or wok over
   medium-high heat. Add the scallions,
   ginger, and garlic. Stir-fry for 30 seconds.
   Add the broth, soy sauce, cider vinegar,
   rice vinegar, and chili powder. Bring to a
   boil, then lower the heat.
2. Add the shrimp and saute for 3–4 minutes,
   just until the shrimp turns pink. Mix
   together the cornstarch or arrowroot
   powder with the water. Add to the skillet
   or wok and cook until thickened. Serve
   the shrimp over the rice.

Preparation time: 20 minutes

Honey-Nut Chicken

Just a few nuts add a crunch and taste to this stir-fry that can't be beat!

6 Servings/Serving Size:
3–4 oz chicken

Exchanges:
1	Starch
3	Very Lean Meat
1	Monounsaturated Fat

Calories	237
Calories from Fat	72
Total Fat	8 g
Saturated Fat	2 g

Cholesterol	69 mg
Sodium	396 mg
Carbohydrate	14 g
Dietary Fiber	2 g
Sugars	9 g

Protein	27 g

Preparation time: 20 minutes

1 Tbsp peanut oil
2 medium carrots, peeled and diagonally
    sliced
2 stalks celery, diagonally sliced
1 1/2 lb boneless, skinless chicken breasts,
    cut into 3-inch strips
1 Tbsp cornstarch or arrowroot powder
3/4 cup fresh orange juice
3 Tbsp lite soy sauce
1 Tbsp honey
1 tsp minced ginger
1/4 cup chopped toasted cashews or peanuts,
    unsalted
1/4 cup minced scallions

1. Heat half of the oil in a wok over high
   heat. Add the carrots and celery and stir-
   fry for 3 minutes. Add the remaining oil
   and chicken breasts and stir-fry for
   5 more minutes.
2. Dissolve the cornstarch or arrowroot
   powder in the orange juice. Mix in the
   soy sauce, honey, and ginger. Add the
   sauce to the wok and cook over medium
   heat until thickened. Top with nuts and
   scallions to serve.

This adapted recipe is courtesy of the National Honey Board.

Korean Chicken

Toast the sesame seeds for this recipe in a dry skillet over medium-high heat for 2–3 minutes, then place in a blender or coffee grinder until crushed.

6 Servings/Serving Size:
3 oz chicken with
1/2 cup rice

Exchanges:

2	Starch
3	Lean Meat

Calories 321
 Calories from Fat . . 89
Total Fat . . . . 10 g
 Saturated Fat . . . . 2 g

Cholesterol . . . . 69 mg
Sodium . . . . . 370 mg
Carbohydrate . . . . 27 g
 Dietary Fiber . . . . . 2 g
 Sugars . . . . 3 g

Protein . . . . 29 g

1 1/2 lb boneless, skinless chicken breasts,
 cut into strips
1 tsp grated fresh ginger
1 Tbsp lite soy sauce
2 Tbsp peanut oil
3 Tbsp crushed toasted sesame seeds
2 scallions, minced
2 garlic cloves, minced
3 cups fresh bean sprouts
3 cups cooked rice
2 Tbsp lite soy sauce

1. In a large bowl, combine the chicken, ginger, and soy sauce. Heat the oil in a wok over high heat. Add the chicken and stir-fry until the chicken is opaque, about 5 minutes.
2. Add sesame seeds, scallions, and garlic and stir-fry for 2 minutes. Add the bean sprouts and cook for 2 minutes. Add the rice and soy sauce, toss well, and serve.

Preparation time: 15 minutes

This adapted recipe is courtesy of the National Broiler Council.

Lemon Chicken

Bean sprouts serve as the "noodles" in this stir-fry.

6 Servings/Serving Size:
3–4 oz chicken

Exchanges:
2	Vegetable
3	Lean Meat

Calories 215
  Calories from Fat . . 68
Total Fat . . . . 8 g
  Saturated Fat . . . . 2 g

Cholesterol . . . . 69 mg
Sodium . . . . . . 171 mg
Carbohydrate . . . . . 9 g
  Dietary Fiber . . . . . 2 g
  Sugars . . . . 4 g

Protein . . . . 27 g

Preparation time: 20 minutes

2 Tbsp sesame oil
3 cups bean sprouts
2 garlic cloves, minced
2 tsp minced ginger
1 1/2 lb boneless, skinless chicken breasts,
  cut into 3-inch strips
1 cup fresh snow peas, trimmed
1/2 cup sliced red pepper
1 Tbsp lite soy sauce
1 Tbsp dry sherry
1 Tbsp fresh lemon juice
1 6-oz can bamboo shoots
1 6-oz can water chestnuts, slivered

1. Heat 1 Tbsp of the oil in a wok over high heat. Add the bean sprouts and stir-fry for 1–2 minutes until crisp. Remove from wok and place on a platter. In the remaining oil, stir-fry the garlic and ginger for 30 seconds. Add the chicken and stir-fry for 4 minutes. Push the chicken up on the sides of the wok.

2. Add the snow peas and red pepper and stir-fry for 2 minutes. Combine the soy sauce, sherry, and lemon juice. Add to the wok along with the bamboo shoots. Add the chicken back to the center of the wok. Cook 2 minutes. Place the chicken over the bean sprouts and top with water chestnuts to serve.

Orange Chicken

This stir-fry is served over aromatic jasmine rice.

6 Servings/Serving Size:
3–4 oz chicken with
1/2 cup rice

Exchanges:

2	Starch
1	Vegetable
3	Very Lean Meat

Calories	296
Calories from Fat	51
Total Fat	6 g
Saturated Fat	1 g

Cholesterol	69 mg
Sodium	269 mg
Carbohydrate	31 g
Dietary Fiber	1 g
Sugars	5 g

Protein	28 g

1 Tbsp canola oil
1 1/2 lb boneless, skinless chicken breasts,
    cut into strips
2 tsp minced ginger
1 cup sliced red pepper
1 cup sliced yellow pepper
1 cup sliced mushrooms
1/4 cup fresh orange juice
1/2 tsp orange extract
2 Tbsp lite soy sauce
2 tsp brown sugar
1/4 cup low-fat, low-sodium chicken broth
1 Tbsp cornstarch or arrowroot powder
3 cups cooked jasmine rice
1/2 cup sliced scallions

1. Heat the oil in a wok over high heat. Add the chicken and stir-fry for 5–6 minutes. Push the chicken up on the sides of the wok. Add the ginger and vegetables to the wok and stir-fry for 6 minutes.
2. Combine remaining ingredients except the rice and scallions, add to the wok, and cook until sauce thickens. Add the chicken back to the center of the wok and cook for 1 minute. Serve over hot rice and garnish with scallions.

Preparation time: 20 minutes

Orange Roughy

Stir-fry orange roughy gently so it doesn't flake into tiny pieces.

6 Servings/Serving Size: 3 oz fish with 1/2 cup rice	
Exchanges:	
2	Starch
1	Vegetable
2	Very Lean Meat
Calories 261	
Calories from Fat . . 32	
Total Fat . . . . 4 g	
Saturated Fat . . . . 1 g	
Cholesterol . . . . 23 mg	
Sodium. . . . . . 408 mg	
Carbohydrate. . . . 34 g	
Dietary Fiber. . . . . 3 g	
Sugars . . . . 5 g	
Protein . . . . 21 g	

Preparation time: 20 minutes

3 tsp peanut oil
2 scallions, minced
3 garlic cloves, minced
2 tsp minced ginger
1 1/2 lb orange roughy, cut into 2-inch cubes
1 cup diagonally sliced carrots
1 cup broccoli florets
1/2 cup sliced red pepper
1/2 cup fresh snow peas, trimmed
3 Tbsp lite soy sauce
2 Tbsp sherry
2 tsp sugar
1/2 cup low-fat, low-sodium chicken broth
2 Tbsp cornstarch or arrowroot powder
3 cups cooked rice

1. Heat 2 tsp of the oil in a wok over medium-high heat. Add the scallions, garlic, and ginger and stir-fry for 1 minute. Add the fish and stir-fry for 3–4 minutes, until it is almost cooked through.

2. Remove the fish from the wok. Add the remaining oil to the wok and stir-fry the carrots for 2 minutes. Add the broccoli and pepper and stir-fry for 4 more minutes. Add the snow peas and stir-fry for 1 minute.

3. Mix together the soy sauce, sherry, sugar, broth, and cornstarch or arrowroot powder. Add the mixture to the wok and stir until sauce has thickened. Add the fish back to the wok and cook for 1 minute. Serve over hot rice.

Penne Pasta

Penne pasta is a welcome surprise in this meatless Asian stir-fry.

6 Servings/Serving Size:
1 cup pasta with
1/2 cup vegetables

Exchanges:
| 3 | Starch |
| 1 | Vegetable |

Calories	262
Calories from Fat	28
Total Fat	3 g
Saturated Fat	0 g

Cholesterol	0 mg
Sodium	374 mg
Carbohydrate	50 g
Dietary Fiber	4 g
Sugars	6 g

| Protein | 9 g |

2 tsp cornstarch or arrowroot powder
3 Tbsp lite soy sauce
3 Tbsp rice vinegar
1 cup low-fat, low-sodium chicken broth
2 tsp canola oil
2 large carrots, thinly sliced
3 garlic cloves, minced
1 cup fresh snow peas, trimmed
1/4 tsp red pepper flakes
6 cups cooked penne pasta
Fresh ground pepper and salt to taste

1. Combine the first four ingredients and set aside. Heat the oil in a large skillet or wok over high heat. Add the carrots and garlic and stir-fry for 5 minutes.
2. Add the snow peas, lower heat to medium-low, and add the red pepper flakes and sauce. Add the pasta to the skillet or wok, bring to a boil, and cook for 2 minutes. Season with pepper and salt to serve.

Preparation time: 20 minutes

Saucy Shrimp and Scallops

Hot chili oil, made with sesame oil and chilies, is available in Asian grocery stores.

6 Servings/Serving Size: 3–4 oz seafood	
Exchanges:	
2	Vegetable
3	Very Lean Meat
Calories 161	
Calories from Fat . . 37	
Total Fat . . . . 4 g	
Saturated Fat . . . . 1 g	
Cholesterol . . . 126 mg	
Sodium . . . . . . 409 mg	
Carbohydrate . . . . . 8 g	
Dietary Fiber . . . . . 2 g	
Sugars . . . . 4 g	
Protein . . . . 23 g	

1 Tbsp hot chili oil
2 garlic cloves, minced
1/4 cup minced scallions
1 small red chili, minced
2 medium carrots, thinly sliced
2 medium stalks celery, thinly sliced
1 lb medium shelled and deveined shrimp
1/2 lb sea scallops
1/4 cup low-fat, low-sodium chicken broth
1/2 cup chopped bok choy cabbage
1/2 cup fresh snow peas, trimmed
2 Tbsp lite soy sauce

1. Heat the oil in a wok over high heat. Add the garlic, scallions, and red chili and stir-fry for 30 seconds. Add the carrots and celery and stir-fry for 3 minutes. Add the shrimp and scallops and stir-fry for 1 minute.
2. Add the broth, cover, and steam for 1 minute. Add the bok choy, snow peas, and soy sauce. Steam for 2 minutes until the snow peas are tender, but still crisp.

Preparation time: 20 minutes

Seafood and Asparagus

You can use shrimp, crab, salmon, swordfish, or tuna in this recipe if you wish.

6 Servings/Serving Size:
3–4 oz seafood with
1/2 cup rice

Exchanges:

2	Starch
1	Vegetable
2	Very Lean Meat

Calories	270
Calories from Fat	36
Total Fat	4 g
Saturated Fat	1 g

Cholesterol	41 mg
Sodium	559 mg
Carbohydrate	34 g
Dietary Fiber	2 g
Sugars	8 g

Protein	24 g

1 Tbsp peanut oil
1 cup thinly sliced red pepper
1/2 cup thinly sliced yellow pepper
1/2 cup diced onion
2 cups sliced fresh asparagus
2 garlic cloves, minced
1 Tbsp minced ginger
1 lb sea scallops
1/2 lb sea bass, cut into 2-inch cubes
1/4 cup lite soy sauce
2 Tbsp rice vinegar
2 tsp sugar
3 cups cooked rice

1. Heat the oil in a wok over high heat. Add the peppers and onion and stir-fry for 3 minutes. Add the asparagus and stir-fry for 3 more minutes. Add the garlic and ginger and stir-fry for 3 minutes.
2. Add the seafood, cover, and steam for 2 minutes. Mix together the soy sauce, rice vinegar, and sugar and add to the wok. Cook for 2–3 minutes and serve over hot rice.

Preparation time: 20 minutes

Southern-Style Pork

This is a decidedly different stir-fry from way down South.

6 Servings/Serving Size: 3–4 oz pork	
Exchanges:	
1	Starch
1/2	Fruit
3	Lean Meat

Calories 272	
Calories from Fat . . 67	
Total Fat . . . . 7 g	
Saturated Fat . . . . 2 g	
Cholesterol . . . . 71 mg	
Sodium . . . . . . 81 mg	
Carbohydrate . . . . 24 g	
Dietary Fiber. . . . . 3 g	
Sugars . . . . 14 g	
Protein . . . . 26 g	

Preparation time: 20 minutes

2 tsp canola oil
1 1/2 lb pork tenderloin, cut into strips
2 medium sweet potatoes, peeled and cut into 4-inch strips
1/2 cup water
1 medium onion, halved and sliced
2 Tbsp raisins
1 Tbsp cornstarch or arrowroot powder
1/4 cup dry white wine
2 cups thinly sliced apple wedges, unpeeled

1. Heat the oil in a skillet or wok over medium-high heat. Add the pork and saute until the pork loses it pinkness, about 6–8 minutes. Remove the pork from the skillet or wok. Add the sweet potatoes and water and cook, covered, for 5 minutes.

2. Return the pork to the skillet or wok, and add the onions and raisins. Continue to saute for 5 minutes. Mix the cornstarch or arrowroot powder and wine together and add to the pork. Cook, stirring, until sauce is thickened. Add the apple wedges and cook for 2–3 more minutes.

This adapted recipe is courtesy of the National Pork Producers.

Southwestern Pork

If you're tired of Asian spices, try this differently flavored stir-fry.

6 Servings/Serving Size: 3 oz pork	
Exchanges:	
2	Vegetable
3	Lean Meat
Calories 212	
Calories from Fat . . 74	
Total Fat . . . . 8 g	
Saturated Fat . . . . 2 g	
Cholesterol . . . . 71 mg	
Sodium . . . . . . 103 mg	
Carbohydrate . . . . . 7 g	
Dietary Fiber . . . . . 1 g	
Sugars . . . . 4 g	
Protein . . . . 26 g	

2 Tbsp dry sherry
2 tsp cornstarch or arrowroot powder
1 tsp cumin
2 garlic cloves, minced
Fresh ground pepper and salt to taste
1 1/2 lb pork tenderloin, cut into 3-inch strips
1 Tbsp canola oil
1 green pepper, seeded and cut into strips
1 medium onion, thinly sliced
12 cherry tomatoes, halved

1. Combine the sherry, cornstarch or arrowroot powder, cumin, garlic, pepper, and salt in a plastic bag. Add the pork slices and shake to coat. Heat the oil in a medium skillet over medium-high heat.
2. Add the pork mixture and stir-fry for 3–4 minutes. Add the remaining ingredients and steam, covered, for 3–5 minutes.

Preparation time: 20 minutes

This adapted recipe is courtesy of the National Pork Producers.

Speedy Steak

Rummage through your refrigerator for these easy stir-fry ingredients!

6 Servings/Serving Size:
3–4 oz meat with
1/2 cup rice

Exchanges:

2	Starch
1	Vegetable
3	Very Lean Meat

Calories 303
  Calories from Fat . . 50
Total Fat . . . . 6 g
  Saturated Fat . . . . 1 g

Cholesterol . . . . 69 mg
Sodium. . . . . . 282 mg
Carbohydrate . . . . 33 g
  Dietary Fiber. . . . . 2 g
  Sugars . . . . 7 g

Protein . . . . 28 g

1 Tbsp canola oil
3 cups sliced raw vegetables (try carrots,
  broccoli, zucchini, and peppers)
2 garlic cloves, minced
1 1/2 lb boneless, skinless chicken breasts or
  lean sirloin steak, cooked and sliced into
  strips
2 Tbsp lite soy sauce
2 Tbsp brown sugar
1 Tbsp dry sherry
3 cups cooked rice
2 Tbsp toasted sesame seeds

1. Heat the oil in a wok over high heat.
   Add the vegetables and stir-fry for
   4 minutes. Add the garlic and stir-fry for
   2 more minutes.
2. Add the chicken or beef and stir-fry
   1 minute. Combine the soy sauce, sugar,
   and sherry and add to the wok. Cover
   and steam for 1 minute. Serve over hot
   rice and garnish with sesame seeds.

Preparation time: 20 minutes

Rice, Potatoes, & Grains

*B*lack Beans and Rice

Try these spicy black beans served with pork.

6 Servings/Serving Size: 1/2 cup	
Exchanges:	
1 1/2	Starch
Calories 115	
Calories from Fat . . . 9	
Total Fat . . . . 1 g	
Saturated Fat . . . . 0 g	
Cholesterol . . . . . 0 mg	
Sodium . . . . . . 103 mg	
Carbohydrate . . . . 22 g	
Dietary Fiber . . . . . 5 g	
Sugars . . . . 2 g	
Protein . . . . 6 g	

1/2 tsp olive oil
1/2 medium onion, chopped
1 garlic clove, minced
1/3 cup short-grain white rice
3/4 cup low-fat, low-sodium chicken broth
1 tsp cumin
1/4 tsp cayenne pepper
1 3/4 cups canned black beans, drained and rinsed

1. Heat the oil in a stockpot over medium-high heat. Add the onion and garlic and saute for 4 minutes. Add the rice and saute for 2 more minutes.
2. Add the chicken broth, bring to a boil, cover, lower the heat, and cook for 20 minutes. Add the spices and the black beans and cook until hot, about 10 minutes.

Preparation time: 20 minutes

Citrus Rice

Cooking rice in chicken broth instead of water guarantees instant flavor.

12 Servings/Serving Size:
1/2 cup

Exchanges:
1 1/2   Starch

Calories 114
  Calories from Fat . . 14
Total Fat . . . . 2 g
  Saturated Fat . . . . 0 g

Cholesterol . . . . . 0 mg
Sodium . . . . . . 44 mg
Carbohydrate . . . . 23 g
  Dietary Fiber . . . . . 1 g
  Sugars . . . . 2 g

Protein . . . . 3 g

Preparation time: 15 minutes

3 1/2 cups low-fat, low-sodium chicken
  broth
1 1/2 cups raw basmati rice, rinsed
2 tsp olive oil
1/4 cup minced onion
1/2 cup each diced red and yellow peppers
2 Tbsp chopped scallions
1/2 cup mandarin oranges, packed in their
  own juice
2 Tbsp orange juice
1 Tbsp lemon juice
Fresh ground pepper and salt to taste

1. In a large pot, bring the broth to a boil.
   Slowly add the rice and return to a boil.
   Cover, reduce heat to low, and cook for
   15–20 minutes until the rice has absorbed
   the broth.
2. Meanwhile, heat the oil in a medium
   skillet over medium-high heat. Add
   the onion and peppers and saute for
   5 minutes. Add the scallions and saute for
   3 more minutes. Add the oranges and
   orange juice and cook for 5 minutes. Add
   the cooked rice, lemon juice, pepper, and
   salt and toss well to serve.

Italian Polenta

Polenta, an Italian dish made with cornmeal, is so popular you can now buy ready-made mixes right in your grocery store.

6 Servings/Serving Size:
One 1-inch square
with sauce

Exchanges:
1 1/2	Starch
1	Vegetable

Calories	138
Calories from Fat . . .	3
Total Fat	0 g
Saturated Fat	0 g

Cholesterol	0 mg
Sodium	471 mg
Carbohydrate	29 g
Dietary Fiber	6 g
Sugars	6 g

Protein	5 g

1 6-oz box polenta mix
1 14-oz can artichoke hearts, packed in
water, chopped
1 16-oz jar marinara sauce
2 Tbsp dry red wine
Nonstick cooking spray

1. Prepare the polenta according to package directions. Place polenta into a 6 x 6-inch baking dish and refrigerate until firm. To make the sauce, combine the remaining ingredients and bring to a boil. Lower the heat and let simmer for 20 minutes.
2. Cut the polenta into even squares. Place on a broiler pan sprayed with nonstick cooking spray and broil for 2–3 minutes. Turn and broil 1–2 more minutes. Serve hot with artichoke sauce on the side.

Preparation time: 20 minutes

Italian Rice Medley

This colorful rice dish goes well with any chicken entree.

6 Servings/Serving Size: 1/2 cup

Exchanges:

2 1/2	Starch
1	Vegetable

Calories	209
Calories from Fat	19
Total Fat	2 g
Saturated Fat	0 g

Cholesterol	0 mg
Sodium	122 mg
Carbohydrate	43 g
Dietary Fiber	2 g
Sugars	3 g

Protein	5 g

2 tsp olive oil
4 scallions, chopped
1 medium red pepper, chopped
1 14-oz can artichoke hearts, packed in
   water, drained and chopped
1 Tbsp minced fresh basil
1 Tbsp minced fresh oregano
1 Tbsp minced fresh Italian parsley
3 cups cooked long-grain rice
2 Tbsp balsamic vinegar

1. Heat the oil in a medium skillet over medium-high heat. Add the scallions and red pepper and saute for 5 minutes.
2. Add the artichokes and herbs and saute for 3 more minutes. Add the rice and drizzle with vinegar to serve.

Preparation time: 15 minutes

Orzo with Herbs

Fresh herbs will make this orzo especially flavorful.

6 Servings/Serving Size: 1 cup	
Exchanges:	
3	Starch
1/2 Monounsaturated Fat	

Calories	254
Calories from Fat	49
Total Fat	5 g
Saturated Fat	1 g
Cholesterol	0 mg
Sodium	25 mg
Carbohydrate	44 g
Dietary Fiber	1 g
Sugars	3 g
Protein	7 g

6 cups hot cooked orzo
2 Tbsp minced fresh basil
1 Tbsp minced fresh rosemary
1 tsp minced fresh oregano
1/2 tsp minced fresh thyme
1/2 tsp minced fresh sage
2 Tbsp minced fresh Italian parsley
2 Tbsp olive oil
1 Tbsp balsamic vinegar
1 tsp lemon juice
Fresh ground pepper and salt to taste

Combine all ingredients and serve at room temperature.

Preparation time: 10 minutes

Orzo with Spinach and Feta Cheese

This dish is a great change from potatoes or rice.

6 Servings/Serving Size: 1/2 cup	
Exchanges:	
2 1/2	Starch
Calories 204	
Calories from Fat . . 30	
Total Fat . . . . 3 g	
Saturated Fat . . . . 1 g	
Cholesterol . . . . . 4 mg	
Sodium . . . . . 82 mg	
Carbohydrate . . . . 37 g	
Dietary Fiber . . . . . 2 g	
Sugars . . . . 4 g	
Protein . . . . 8 g	

1 1/2 cups dry orzo
2 tsp olive oil
1 medium onion, minced
1 10-oz package frozen chopped spinach, thawed and well drained
1/4 cup crumbled feta cheese
Fresh ground pepper to taste

1. Cook the orzo according to package directions. Drain. Heat the oil in a skillet over medium-high heat. Add the onion and saute for 5 minutes. Add the spinach and saute for 4 more minutes.
2. Toss the onion and spinach mixture with the hot orzo. Add the feta cheese and ground pepper and toss well. Serve immediately.

Preparation time: 15 minutes

Parmesan Risotto

Risotto was meant to be eaten very fresh, so serve this dish immediately after cooking it.

6 Servings/Serving Size:
1/2 cup

Exchanges:
2 1/2   Starch
1/2 Monounsaturated Fat

Calories 226
  Calories from Fat . . 55
Total Fat . . . . 6 g
  Saturated Fat . . . . 2 g

Cholesterol . . . . . 6 mg
Sodium . . . . . . 200 mg
Carbohydrate . . . . 36 g
  Dietary Fiber . . . . . 2 g
  Sugars . . . . 4 g

Protein . . . . 8 g

1 Tbsp olive oil
1 1/2 cups minced onion
1 1/3 cups Arborio rice
1/2 cup dry white wine
4 cups low-fat, low-sodium chicken broth, hot
1/2 tsp turmeric
1/2 cup Parmesan cheese
1/2 cup minced fresh parsley

1. Heat the oil in a large stockpot. Add the onion and saute for 5–8 minutes. Add the rice and saute for 3 more minutes. Add the wine and cook until the wine is absorbed.
2. Add one cup of the hot chicken broth and stir until the rice has absorbed the broth. Continue to add cups of broth until the rice absorbs each cup. Add the turmeric during the last cup of broth. Add the cheese and parsley and serve.

Preparation time: 15 minutes

Quick Hoppin' John

Hoppin' John is a nutritious blend of black-eyed peas, rice, and vegetables. (If you need to substitute regular turkey for the smoked turkey in this recipe, use the nutrient analysis in parentheses.)

6 Servings/Serving Size: 1 cup	
Exchanges:	
3	Starch
1	Vegetable
1	Very Lean Meat
Calories.... 292 (299)	
Calories from Fat.. 38	
Total Fat .... 4 g	
Saturated Fat .... 1 g	
Cholesterol..... 7 mg (12 mg)	
Sodium...... 392 mg (229 mg)	
Carbohydrate.... 51 g	
Dietary Fiber..... 8 g	
Sugars .... 6 g	
Protein ... 15 g (16 g)	

1 Tbsp canola oil
1 medium onion, chopped
1/2 cup diced carrots
1/2 cup diced celery
2 garlic cloves, minced
2 15-oz cans black-eyed peas, drained
1 tsp minced fresh thyme
1/2 lb fresh collard greens, stems removed, washed, and torn (or 2 packages frozen collard greens, thawed slightly)
1 cup white rice
2 1/2 cups low-fat, low-sodium chicken broth
1/2 cup diced smoked turkey breast (or regular diced turkey)
Fresh ground pepper to taste

1. Heat the oil in a stockpot over medium-high heat. Add the onion and carrots and saute for 5 minutes. Add the celery and garlic and saute for 3 more minutes.
2. Add the black-eyed peas, thyme, collard greens, and rice. Saute for 2 minutes. Add the chicken broth and bring to a boil.
3. Cover and lower the heat for 20 minutes, until water is absorbed and rice is tender. Add the turkey and cook 5 more minutes. Season with pepper to serve.

Preparation time: 20 minutes

Quinoa Stuffing

Quinoa is a high-protein, high-fiber grain—and it only takes 15 minutes to prepare! Look for quinoa in natural food stores. It is very important to rinse quinoa well. This removes some of the bitterness naturally present in the outside ring of the grain. Quinoa stuffing is best served separately in a casserole dish instead of baked in a bird.

6 Servings/Serving Size:
1/2 cup

Exchanges:
2	Starch
1	Vegetable
1/2	Monounsaturated Fat

Calories 205
  Calories from Fat . . 47
Total Fat . . . . 5 g
  Saturated Fat . . . . 1 g

Cholesterol . . . . . 0 mg
Sodium . . . . . . 82 mg
Carbohydrate . . . . 35 g
  Dietary Fiber . . . . . 4 g
  Sugars . . . . 3 g

Protein . . . . 8 g

1 1/2 cups dry quinoa, rinsed well
3 cups low-fat, low-sodium chicken broth
2 tsp olive oil
1 medium onion, diced
2 garlic cloves, minced
1/2 cup diced celery
1/2 cup diced carrots
1/2 cup minced scallions
Fresh ground pepper to taste

1. In a medium saucepan, bring the broth to a boil. Add the rinsed quinoa and return to a boil. Lower the heat, cover, and cook for about 15 minutes until all the water is absorbed.
2. Meanwhile, heat the oil in a skillet over medium-high heat. Add the onion and garlic and saute for 5 minutes. Add the celery and carrots and saute for 5 minutes.
3. Add the scallions and saute for 2 minutes. Combine the vegetables with the quinoa and grind in pepper to serve.

Preparation time: 17 minutes

Sweet Potato and Turnip Swirl

This combination of sweet potatoes and spicy turnips could make turnip lovers out of us all!

6 Servings/Serving Size: 1/2 cup	
Exchanges:	
1	Starch
Calories 73	
Calories from Fat . . . 9	
Total Fat . . . . 1 g	
Saturated Fat . . . . 0 g	
Cholesterol . . . . . 0 mg	
Sodium . . . . . . 34 mg	
Carbohydrate . . . . 16 g	
Dietary Fiber . . . . . 2 g	
Sugars . . . . 8 g	
Protein . . . . 1 g	

1/2 lb turnips, peeled and cubed
2 medium sweet potatoes (about 13 oz), peeled and cubed
1 tsp minced ginger
1 Tbsp low-calorie margarine
1 Tbsp sugar
2 tsp grated orange peel

1. In a medium saucepan, cook the turnips and sweet potatoes in boiling water to cover for about 15–20 minutes until soft. Drain. Transfer to a food processor and puree.
2. In a saucepan, combine the ginger, margarine, sugar, and orange peel. Add the puree and toss to coat with the margarine mixture. Serve warm.

Preparation time: 15 minutes

Vegetables

*A*pple-Glazed Baby Carrots

No need for sticky brown sugar and high-fat butter—let the natural, sweet taste of the carrots shine through.

6 Servings/Serving Size:
1/2 cup

Exchanges:
2   Vegetable

Calories 61
  Calories from Fat . . 12
Total Fat . . . . 1 g
  Saturated Fat . . . . 0 g

Cholesterol . . . . . 0 mg
Sodium . . . . . . 77 mg
Carbohydrate . . . . 12 g
  Dietary Fiber . . . . . 2 g
  Sugars . . . . 7 g

Protein . . . . 1 g

3 cups baby carrots (about 1 1/2 bags)
1 Tbsp lemon juice
1 Tbsp low-calorie margarine
3 Tbsp apple juice concentrate
2/3 cup low-fat, low-sodium chicken broth
1 tsp cinnamon
2 tsp cornstarch or arrowroot powder
1 tsp water

1. In a steamer over 2 inches of boiling water, steam the carrots, covered, for 3 minutes. Sprinkle with lemon juice. Melt the margarine in a medium skillet over medium heat. Add the apple juice concentrate and cook until it melts.
2. Add the broth and cinnamon and bring to a boil. Mix together the cornstarch or arrowroot powder with the water. Add to the skillet, lower the heat, and cook until thickened. Add the carrots and toss well to coat.

Preparation time: 15 minutes

Asparagus Vinaigrette

Delightfully crunchy, asparagus also tastes great cold.

6 Servings/Serving Size: 1/2 cup	
Exchanges:	
1	Vegetable
1	Monounsaturated Fat
Calories 60	
Calories from Fat . . 44	
Total Fat . . . . 5 g	
Saturated Fat . . . . 1 g	
Cholesterol . . . . . 0 mg	
Sodium . . . . . . 73 mg	
Carbohydrate . . . . . 4 g	
Dietary Fiber . . . . . 1 g	
Sugars . . . . 2 g	
Protein . . . . 2 g	

1 1/2 lb fresh asparagus
1/3 cup balsamic vinegar
2 Tbsp low-fat, low-sodium chicken broth
2 Tbsp olive oil
2 tsp lemon juice
2 Tbsp Dijon mustard
2 Tbsp minced fresh parsley
2 tsp minced fresh tarragon
1 Tbsp minced fresh chives

1. Snap the tough ends off the asparagus. Steam the asparagus in a metal steamer over boiling water for 5–8 minutes, until asparagus is tender-crisp and bright green.
2. Drain the asparagus and splash cold water over it to stop the cooking process. Set aside. Combine all remaining ingredients to make the vinaigrette, pour the vinaigrette over the asparagus, and serve.

Preparation time: 15 minutes

Baked Vegetable Casserole

This one-pot side dish will stick to your ribs on cold winter days.

6 Servings/Serving Size: 1/2 cup	
Exchanges:	
1 1/2	Starch
Calories	123
Calories from Fat	19
Total Fat	2 g
Saturated Fat	0 g
Cholesterol	3 mg
Sodium	555 mg
Carbohydrate	22 g
Dietary Fiber	3 g
Sugars	6 g
Protein	5 g

1/2 cup evaporated fat-free milk
3 cups frozen mixed vegetables, thawed slightly
1 11-oz can reduced-fat cream of mushroom soup
1 Tbsp Dijon mustard
1 tsp minced garlic
1 tsp dill
1/2 cup dry bread crumbs

Preheat the oven to 350 degrees. Mix all ingredients together except the bread crumbs and place in a 9-inch glass casserole dish. Sprinkle the bread crumbs over the top and bake for 30 minutes.

Preparation time: 15 minutes

Broccoli with Sun-Dried Tomatoes and Pine Nuts

6 Servings/Serving Size: 1/2 cup	
Exchanges:	
2	Vegetable
1	Fat
Calories 95	
Calories from Fat . . 50	
Total Fat . . . . 6 g	
Saturated Fat . . . . 1 g	
Cholesterol . . . . . 0 mg	
Sodium . . . . . . 140 mg	
Carbohydrate . . . . 10 g	
Dietary Fiber . . . . . 4 g	
Sugars . . . . 3 g	
Protein . . . . 5 g	

Preparation time: 15 minutes

1 1/2 lb fresh broccoli (stems sliced and separated into florets)
2 tsp olive oil
1/2 cup diced red onion
10 sun-dried tomatoes, rehydrated
1/2 cup low-fat, low-sodium chicken broth
1 Tbsp fresh lemon juice
1/4 cup toasted pine nuts

1. Fill a large stockpot with water and bring to a boil. Add the broccoli and boil gently for 1 minute. Drain. Plunge the broccoli into a bowl of ice water. Drain again and set aside.
2. Heat the oil in a saucepan over medium-high heat. Add the red onion and saute for 5 minutes. Dice the sun-dried tomatoes and add to the onion. Add the broth and bring to a boil. Lower the heat, cover, and let steam for 2 minutes.
3. Add the lemon juice to the tomato mixture. Add the broccoli and stir well to coat it with the tomatoes and onion. Place broccoli in a serving bowl, top with toasted pine nuts, and serve.

*B*russels Sprouts and Water Chestnuts

Although Brussels sprouts usually make their way to holiday tables, this fiber-rich vegetable should be served all winter long.

6 Servings/Serving Size: 1/2 cup	
Exchanges:	
1	Starch
1	Vegetable
1/2	Monounsaturated Fat

Calories	126
Calories from Fat	29
Total Fat	3 g
Saturated Fat	0 g

Cholesterol	0 mg
Sodium	50 mg
Carbohydrate	23 g
Dietary Fiber	4 g
Sugars	8 g

Protein	4 g

3 cups Brussels sprouts
1 cup sliced water chestnuts
1 orange, peeled, separated into sections, and seeded
1/2 cup low-fat, low-sodium chicken broth
1 Tbsp canola oil
Fresh ground pepper and salt to taste

1. Trim each sprout by cutting a little piece off the bottom. With a small paring knife, make an "X" in the top of the sprout. Repeat with all sprouts. In a steamer over 2 inches of boiling water, steam the sprouts, covered, for about 10 minutes.
2. Remove the steamed sprouts from the pot. Let cool. Cut each sprout in half and place in a casserole dish. Layer the chestnuts on top of the sprouts. Place the orange sections on top of the chestnuts.
3. Pour the broth over all ingredients. Drizzle the casserole with oil. Grind in pepper and add salt. Bake in a preheated 350-degree oven for 15 minutes, until the oranges are soft.

Preparation time: 20 minutes

Carrots and Shallots with Fresh Herbs

It's important that fresh herbs be added last in the cooking process. High heat may destroy their delicate flavors.

6 Servings/Serving Size: 1/2 cup	
Exchanges:	
1	Vegetable
1/2 Monounsaturated Fat	
Calories 58	
Calories from Fat . . 23	
Total Fat . . . . 3 g	
Saturated Fat . . . . 0 g	
Cholesterol . . . . . 0 mg	
Sodium . . . . . . 79 mg	
Carbohydrate . . . . . 9 g	
Dietary Fiber . . . . . 3 g	
Sugars . . . . 3 g	
Protein . . . . 1 g	

1 lb baby carrots
1 Tbsp olive oil
1/4 cup chopped shallots
1/2 cup low-fat, low-sodium chicken broth
1 tsp lemon juice
1/2 cup water
Fresh ground pepper and salt to taste
1 1/2 Tbsp minced fresh parsley
1/2 Tbsp minced fresh dill
1 tsp minced fresh rosemary

Combine all ingredients except the herbs in a saucepan and cook over medium heat until carrots are tender, about 5–8 minutes. Add the fresh herbs and toss well; cook for 1 more minute.

Preparation time: 10 minutes

Cauliflower with Low-Fat Cheese Sauce

Tender cauliflower gets a little flavor boost from this creamy cheese sauce.

Preparation time: 15 minutes

1 medium cauliflower, broken into florets (about 3 cups)
2 Tbsp low-calorie margarine
1 Tbsp unbleached flour
1 cup evaporated fat-free milk
1/4 cup low-fat cheddar cheese
2 Tbsp low-fat cottage cheese
2 tsp Parmesan cheese
1 tsp paprika
Fresh ground pepper and salt to taste

1. Steam the cauliflower in a steamer over boiling water, covered, for 5–6 minutes until the florets just turn tender. Set aside. Melt the margarine in a medium skillet over medium heat. Add the flour and stir until smooth.
2. Add the milk and cook over medium-low heat until slightly thickened. Add the cheeses. Cook until cheeses melt, about 3 minutes. (Add a little liquid if the sauce is too thick.) Add the paprika, pepper, and salt. Pour the sauce over steamed cauliflower and serve.

Corn and Pepper Saute

This corn medley can be served hot or cold.

6 Servings/Serving Size: 1/2 cup	
Exchanges:	
1	Starch
Calories 71	
Calories from Fat . . 23	
Total Fat . . . . 3 g	
Saturated Fat . . . . 0 g	
Cholesterol . . . . . 0 mg	
Sodium . . . . . 29 mg	
Carbohydrate . . . . 13 g	
Dietary Fiber. . . . . 2 g	
Sugars . . . . 3 g	
Protein . . . . 2 g	

1 Tbsp canola oil
1/2 cup chopped onion
1 1/2 cups corn (scrape right off the cob, or use frozen and thawed)
1/2 cup diced red pepper
1/2 cup diced green pepper
1/2 cup halved cherry tomatoes
2 Tbsp fresh lemon juice
2 Tbsp minced fresh basil
Fresh ground pepper and salt to taste

1. Heat the oil in a large skillet over medium-high heat. Add the onion and saute for 5 minutes. Add the corn and peppers and saute for 5 more minutes.
2. Add the cherry tomatoes and lemon juice. Cover and cook for 3 minutes. Add in basil, black pepper, and salt and cook 1 more minute.

Preparation time: 15 minutes

Creamy Peas and Corn

This colorful combination is great served with grilled meats. Try using corn scraped right off the cob if you can.

6 Servings/Serving Size: 1/2 cup	
Exchanges:	
1 1/2	Starch
Calories	124
Calories from Fat	19
Total Fat	2 g
Saturated Fat	0 g
Cholesterol	2 mg
Sodium	113 mg
Carbohydrate	21 g
Dietary Fiber	3 g
Sugars	7 g
Protein	7 g

1 1/2 cups peas
1 1/2 cups corn kernels
2 Tbsp low-calorie margarine
1/2 cup minced shallots
1/2 cup minced red pepper
1 cup evaporated fat-free milk
2 Tbsp sherry
1 Tbsp cornstarch or arrowroot powder
2 Tbsp water
2 Tbsp minced fresh parsley

1. Cook fresh peas in boiling water for 5 minutes and drain. If you are using frozen peas, cook according to package directions.
2. If you are using fresh corn, just scrape the kernels off the cob after removing the corn silks and boil gently for 1 minute. If you are using frozen corn, defrost it completely and drain.
3. Melt the margarine in a saucepan over medium-high heat. Add the shallots and red pepper and saute for 5 minutes. Add the milk and sherry and simmer for 5 more minutes.
4. Combine the cornstarch or arrowroot powder and the water and add to the sauce. Cook over medium heat until bubbly. Add the corn and peas, and garnish with parsley to serve.

Preparation time: 15 minutes

Creamy Tarragon Asparagus

Tarragon, a licorice-flavored herb, is very popular in French cuisine. It tastes great in this creamy sauce poured over freshly steamed asparagus.

6 Servings/Serving Size: 1/2 cup	
Exchanges:	
2	Vegetable
1/2	Saturated Fat
Calories 78	
Calories from Fat . . 28	
Total Fat . . . . 3 g	
Saturated Fat . . . . 2 g	
Cholesterol . . . . 10 mg	
Sodium . . . . . . 152 mg	
Carbohydrate . . . . . 8 g	
Dietary Fiber . . . . . 2 g	
Sugars . . . . 5 g	
Protein . . . . 6 g	

2 1/2 lb fresh asparagus, ends snapped off
1/2 cup low-fat sour cream
1/4 cup Parmesan cheese
1 Tbsp low-fat mayonnaise
1 Tbsp tarragon
1 Tbsp lemon juice
1/2 cup evaporated fat-free milk
Fresh ground pepper and salt to taste

1. Rinse the asparagus and pat dry. Steam the spears in an asparagus steamer or in a metal steamer over boiling water for 8 minutes until tender-crisp.
2. Meanwhile, combine all remaining ingredients in a saucepan. Bring to a boil, lower the heat, and simmer for 5 minutes. Pour the sauce over the asparagus and serve.

Preparation time: 15 minutes

Dilled Carrots

Carrots and dill make a wonderful pair.

6 Servings/Serving Size: 1/2 cup

Exchanges:
1	Vegetable
1/2 Monounsaturated Fat	

Calories	 46
Calories from Fat	. . 14
Total Fat	. . . . 2 g
Saturated Fat	. . . . 0 g

Cholesterol	. . . . . 0 mg
Sodium	. . . . . 101 mg
Carbohydrate	. . . . . 8 g
Dietary Fiber	. . . . . 2 g
Sugars	. . . . 3 g

Protein	. . . . 1 g

3 cups sliced carrots or whole baby carrots
1/2 tsp lemon pepper
2 tsp minced fresh dill
2 tsp olive oil
Fresh ground pepper and salt to taste

Steam the carrots until tender, about 5–8 minutes. Combine with the other ingredients and serve.

Preparation time: 10 minutes

*F*resh Peas with Tarragon

Fresh is always best, but you can use frozen and thawed peas in this recipe if you need to.

6 Servings/Serving Size: 1/2 cup	
Exchanges:	
1	Starch
Calories 89	
Calories from Fat . . 16	
Total Fat . . . . 2 g	
Saturated Fat . . . . 1 g	
Cholesterol . . . . . 4 mg	
Sodium . . . . . . 181 mg	
Carbohydrate . . . . 14 g	
Dietary Fiber . . . . . 5 g	
Sugars . . . . 6 g	
Protein . . . . 5 g	

3 cups peas
1 Tbsp tarragon vinegar
2 tsp butter
1/2 cup pearl onions
1/2 cup low-fat, low-sodium chicken broth
1/4 tsp minced fresh tarragon

Combine all ingredients except tarragon in a saucepan and cook over medium heat until peas and onions are tender, about 5–8 minutes. (Allow a little more cooking time if you are using fresh shelled peas.) Add the tarragon, toss lightly, and serve.

Preparation time: 10 minutes

Garden Vegetable Stir-Fry

The whole garden's in this fiber-packed side dish!

6 Servings/Serving Size: 1/2 cup	
Exchanges:	
2	Vegetable
Calories 45	
Calories from Fat . . . 6	
Total Fat . . . . 1 g	
Saturated Fat . . . . 0 g	
Cholesterol . . . . . 0 mg	
Sodium . . . . . . 355 mg	
Carbohydrate . . . . . 9 g	
Dietary Fiber . . . . . 3 g	
Sugars . . . . 4 g	
Protein . . . . 3 g	

1 cup low-fat, low-sodium chicken broth
2 garlic cloves, minced
2 tsp minced ginger
2 scallions, minced
1 cup broccoli florets
1 cup cauliflower florets
2 medium carrots, peeled and diagonally sliced
1 small red pepper, cored, seeded, and sliced thin
3 Tbsp lite soy sauce
2 Tbsp lemon juice

1. Heat the broth in a wok or heavy skillet over medium-high heat. Add the garlic, ginger, and scallions and stir-fry for 3 minutes.
2. Add the broccoli, cauliflower, and carrots and stir-fry for 5 minutes. Add the red pepper, soy sauce, and lemon juice. Cover and steam for 5 minutes.

Preparation time: 15 minutes

Ginger-Glazed Carrots

These carrots have a delicate Asian flavor.

6 Servings/Serving Size: 1 large carrot	
Exchanges:	
1	Vegetable
Calories 66	
Calories from Fat . . . 8	
Total Fat . . . . 1 g	
Saturated Fat . . . . 0 g	
Cholesterol . . . . . 0 mg	
Sodium . . . . . . 234 mg	
Carbohydrate . . . . 14 g	
Dietary Fiber . . . . . 4 g	
Sugars . . . . 6 g	
Protein . . . . 2 g	

6 large carrots, peeled and sliced in half
   lengthwise
3 Tbsp lite soy sauce
3 Tbsp rice vinegar
2 garlic cloves, minced
2 tsp sesame oil
2 tsp minced ginger
1/4 tsp Chinese Five Spice

1. In a large pot of boiling water, add the carrots and parboil for 5 minutes. Drain and rinse with cold water. In a large glass dish, combine the remaining ingredients. Add the carrots and marinate for 30 minutes.
2. Prepare an outdoor grill with an oiled rack set 4 inches from the heat source. On a gas grill, set the heat to high. Using an oiled, wire-hinged vegetable basket or grilling directly on the rack (whichever you find easier), cook the carrots, turning constantly, for 10 minutes, until they are slightly charred.

Preparation time: 10 minutes

Herbed Tomato Sauce with Sauted Vegetables

The secret to this tomato sauce is horseradish. Its unique flavor makes a vegetable side dish into a real crowd-pleaser. Or try serving the sauce over pasta or brown rice.

6 Servings/Serving Size: 1/2 cup

Exchanges:

1	Vegetable
1/2	Monounsaturated Fat

Calories 41
Calories from Fat . . 16
Total Fat . . . . 2 g
Saturated Fat . . . . 0 g

Cholesterol . . . . . 0 mg
Sodium . . . . . . 11 mg
Carbohydrate. . . . . 6 g
Dietary Fiber. . . . . 2 g
Sugars . . . . 4 g

Protein . . . . 1 g

2 medium tomatoes, seeded and pureed in a blender
1 1/2 Tbsp prepared horseradish
2 Tbsp dry red wine
1 tsp sugar
2 tsp olive oil
2 garlic cloves, minced
1 tsp minced fresh basil
1/2 tsp minced fresh thyme
2 small zucchini, sliced into 1/4-inch-thick rounds
1/2 cup sliced fresh mushrooms
1/2 cup halved cherry tomatoes

1. In a small bowl, combine the pureed tomatoes, horseradish, wine, and sugar. Heat the oil in a large saucepan over medium-high heat. Add the garlic and saute for 30 seconds. Raise the heat slightly, add the basil and thyme, and stir-fry for 30 seconds.
2. Lower the heat slightly, add the zucchini and mushrooms, and saute for 2 minutes. Add the cherry tomatoes and pureed tomato mixture and cook, covered, over medium-low heat for 5 minutes.

Preparation time: 15 minutes

This adapted recipe is courtesy of the Horseradish Information Council.

Honey-Grilled Vidalia Onions

Vidalia onions are so sweet they can be eaten like apples!

6 Servings/Serving Size: 1/2 onion	
Exchanges:	
1	Starch
Calories 67	
Calories from Fat . . . 8	
Total Fat . . . . 1 g	
Saturated Fat . . . . 0 g	
Cholesterol . . . . . 0 mg	
Sodium . . . . . 205 mg	
Carbohydrate . . . . 15 g	
Dietary Fiber . . . . . 1 g	
Sugars . . . . 11 g	
Protein . . . . 2 g	

1 Tbsp honey
1/2 cup rice vinegar
2 Tbsp lite soy sauce
1 tsp sesame oil
3 large Vidalia onions, peeled

1. Combine the first four ingredients to make the honey sauce. Prepare an outside grill with an oiled rack set 6 inches above the heat source. On a gas grill, set the heat to medium.
2. Cut 3 6-inch pieces of aluminum foil. Place the onions on the foil. Brush each onion with the honey sauce. Fold the foil into a package around the onion and grill for about 30 minutes until the onions are soft. Remove the onions from the foil, cut in half, and serve.

Preparation time: 10 minutes

Mushroom and Asparagus Toss

For a more exotic flavor, try to use a different mushroom like shiitake or cremini in this recipe.

6 Servings/Serving Size: 1/2 cup

Exchanges:
1	Vegetable
1/2	Monounsaturated Fat

Calories 50
Calories from Fat . . 31
Total Fat . . . . 3 g
  Saturated Fat . . . . 0 g

Cholesterol . . . . . 0 mg
Sodium . . . . . . 38 mg
Carbohydrate . . . . . 4 g
  Dietary Fiber . . . . . 2 g
  Sugars . . . . 1 g

Protein . . . . 2 g

1 Tbsp olive oil
2 garlic cloves, minced
1/4 cup minced scallions
1 1/2 cups sliced fresh asparagus
1 1/2 cups sliced mushrooms
1/2 cup low-fat, low-sodium chicken broth
Fresh ground pepper and salt to taste
1 Tbsp chopped toasted walnuts

1. Heat the oil in a skillet over medium-high heat. Add the garlic and scallions and saute for 30 seconds. Add the asparagus and mushrooms and saute for 5 minutes.
2. Add the broth, cover, and steam for 3 minutes. Season with ground pepper and salt and garnish with toasted walnuts to serve.

Preparation time: 20 minutes

*R*aisin Carrots

This is a deliciously sweet vegetable dish.

6 Servings/Serving Size: 1/2 cup	
Exchanges:	
2	Vegetable
1/2 Monounsaturated Fat	
Calories 62	
Calories from Fat . . 21	
Total Fat . . . . 2 g	
Saturated Fat . . . . 0 g	
Cholesterol . . . . . 0 mg	
Sodium . . . . . . 48 mg	
Carbohydrate . . . . 10 g	
Dietary Fiber . . . . . 3 g	
Sugars . . . . 5 g	
Protein . . . . 1 g	

1 Tbsp olive oil
2 Tbsp red wine vinegar
1 Tbsp minced fresh Italian parsley
2 tsp cumin
1/2 Tbsp minced fresh cilantro
2 Tbsp golden raisins
3 cups baby carrots, steamed until tender

Whisk together the dressing ingredients.
Combine with the cooked carrots and serve.

Preparation time: 10 minutes

Roasted Asparagus and Garlic

You may want to roast this aromatic vegetable dish at the same time as your dinner meat.

6 Servings/Serving Size: 1/2 cup	
Exchanges:	
1	Vegetable
1	Monounsaturated Fat
Calories 72	
Calories from Fat . . 43	
Total Fat . . . . 5 g	
Saturated Fat . . . . 1 g	
Cholesterol . . . . . 0 mg	
Sodium . . . . . . 34 mg	
Carbohydrate . . . . . 6 g	
Dietary Fiber . . . . . 2 g	
Sugars . . . . 3 g	
Protein . . . . 3 g	

12 garlic cloves
2 Tbsp olive oil
1/4 cup dry white wine
3 cups sliced fresh asparagus
6 fresh thyme sprigs
Fresh ground pepper and salt to taste

Preheat the oven to 350 degrees. Tear off 6 large pieces of aluminum foil. Divide all the ingredients on each piece of foil. Fold over each foil packet to seal it. Place the packets on a baking sheet and roast in the oven for 25–30 minutes until the asparagus is tender.

Preparation time: 10 minutes

Sugar Snap Peas and Peppers

The crunch of this dish is a welcome surprise.

6 Servings/Serving Size: 1/2 cup

Exchanges:
1	Vegetable
1/2	Monounsaturated Fat

Calories 40
  Calories from Fat . . 22
Total Fat . . . . 2 g
  Saturated Fat . . . . 0 g

Cholesterol . . . . . 0 mg
Sodium . . . . . . 227 mg
Carbohydrate . . . . . 5 g
  Dietary Fiber . . . . . 1 g
  Sugars . . . . 2 g

Protein . . . . 1 g

1 Tbsp canola oil
1 1/2 cups sugar snap peas (do not shell)
1/2 cup each julienned red, yellow, and
  green peppers
2 Tbsp lite soy sauce
1 Tbsp lemon juice
Fresh ground pepper and salt to taste

Heat the oil in a skillet over medium-high heat. Add the peas and peppers and saute for 5 minutes. Sprinkle with soy sauce and lemon juice. Grind in pepper and salt to serve.

Preparation time: 15 minutes

Summer Squash with Golden Raisins

This all-golden side dish is slightly sweet.

6 Servings/Serving Size: 1/2 cup

Exchanges:

1/2	Fruit
1	Vegetable

Calories	59
Calories from Fat	2
Total Fat	0 g
Saturated Fat	0 g

Cholesterol	0 mg
Sodium	2 mg
Carbohydrate	15 g
Dietary Fiber	1 g
Sugars	12 g

Protein	1 g

2 cups sliced summer squash (1/4-inch-thick slices)
1/2 cup golden raisins
1/2 cup sliced golden delicious apples (leave skin on)
1/2 cup water
2 tsp cinnamon
2 tsp honey

Combine all ingredients in a saucepan. Cook over medium-low heat for about 8 minutes until the squash and apples are tender.

Preparation time: 10 minutes

Vegetable Medley

This is a quick way to spice up frozen vegetables.

6 Servings/Serving Size: 1/2 cup	
Exchanges:	
1	Vegetable
1/2	Fat
Calories 45	
Calories from Fat . . 11	
Total Fat . . . . 1 g	
Saturated Fat . . . . 0 g	
Cholesterol . . . . . 0 mg	
Sodium . . . . . 127 mg	
Carbohydrate . . . . . 5 g	
Dietary Fiber . . . . . 1 g	
Sugars . . . . 3 g	
Protein . . . . 1 g	

1 1-lb bag frozen vegetable medley (including sugar snap peas, carrots, onions, and mushrooms)
1/2 cup low-fat, low-sodium chicken broth
1 Tbsp low-calorie margarine
1 Tbsp minced fresh herb of choice (try basil, oregano, thyme, or chervil)
1 tsp lemon pepper
Salt to taste

Steam the frozen vegetables in the broth until tender. Remove the vegetables and reduce the liquid in the pot to 2 Tbsp. Add the margarine, minced herb, and lemon pepper. Drizzle over the vegetables and serve.

Preparation time: 15 minutes

Zesty Mexican Cauliflower

The sauce in this recipe is great over a baked potato, too.

6 Servings/Serving Size: 1/2 cup	
Exchanges:	
1	Starch
Calories 77	
Calories from Fat . . 21	
Total Fat . . . . 2 g	
Saturated Fat . . . . 1 g	
Cholesterol . . . . . 8 mg	
Sodium . . . . . . 129 mg	
Carbohydrate . . . . 12 g	
Dietary Fiber . . . . . 2 g	
Sugars . . . . 3 g	
Protein . . . . 4 g	

1 1/2 cups cauliflower florets
1/2 cup low-fat sour cream
1 Tbsp low-fat mayonnaise
1 tsp hot pepper sauce
1/2 cup salsa
1/4 cup low-fat shredded Cheddar cheese
1 1/2 cups cooked fresh corn

1. Cook the cauliflower florets by steaming them over boiling water for 5 minutes until tender. Drain and set aside.
2. Combine all sauce ingredients in a large saucepan and cook over medium heat until bubbly, stirring constantly. Add the cooked cauliflower and corn. Toss well and serve.

Preparation time: 15 minutes

Zucchini Mexican Style

Chili powder and cumin spice up fresh zucchini.

6 Servings/Serving Size:
1/2 cup

Exchanges:
1   Vegetable
1/2 Monounsaturated Fat

Calories 51
  Calories from Fat . . 22
Total Fat . . . . 2 g
  Saturated Fat . . . . 0 g

Cholesterol . . . . . 0 mg
Sodium . . . . . 13 mg
Carbohydrate . . . . 8 g
  Dietary Fiber . . . . . 2 g
  Sugars . . . . 4 g

Protein . . . . 1 g

1 Tbsp olive oil
1 Tbsp cumin seeds
1 medium onion, minced
3 garlic cloves, minced
1 1/2 cups sliced zucchini (1/4-inch-thick
   slices)
1/2 cup diced tomatoes
1/4 cup corn
3 Tbsp lime juice
2 tsp chili powder
Fresh ground pepper to taste

1. Heat the oil in a large skillet over medium-high heat. Add the cumin seeds and roast for 30 seconds. Add the onion and saute for 5 minutes. Add the garlic and saute for 3 more minutes.
2. Add the zucchini and saute for 2 minutes. Add the tomatoes and corn and saute for 2 more minutes. Add the lime juice and chili powder; cover and cook for 2 minutes. Grind in pepper and serve.

Preparation time: 15 minutes

*B*runches

Apple Raisin Pancakes

Leftover pancakes from this breakfast make a great snack, too.

6 Servings/Serving Size: 2 pancakes	
Exchanges:	
1 1/2	Starch
1	Fruit
Calories 196	
Calories from Fat . . 19	
Total Fat . . . . 2 g	
Saturated Fat . . . . 1 g	
Cholesterol . . . . 71 mg	
Sodium . . . . . . 145 mg	
Carbohydrate . . . . 40 g	
Dietary Fiber . . . . . 3 g	
Sugars . . . . 14 g	
Protein . . . . 6 g	

2 eggs, beaten
1 cup unsweetened applesauce
1 tsp cinnamon
2 tsp sugar
1 cup unbleached white flour
1/2 cup whole-wheat flour
2 tsp baking powder
2 tsp vanilla
1/2 cup golden raisins

Combine all ingredients until blended. Cook on a nonstick griddle over medium heat until both sides are browned, about 5–7 minutes.

Preparation time: 10 minutes

Asian Frittata

You can serve this nutritious meal for a light lunch, too.

6 Servings/Serving Size: 1 wedge	
Exchanges:	
2	Vegetable
2	Very Lean Meat

Calories	125
Calories from Fat	28
Total Fat	3 g
Saturated Fat	1 g
Cholesterol	0 mg
Sodium	426 mg
Carbohydrate	9 g
Dietary Fiber	1 g
Sugars	5 g
Protein	15 g

1 Tbsp peanut oil
3 scallions, minced
2 tsp grated fresh ginger
2 garlic cloves, minced
1 cup diced red pepper
12 egg substitutes
2 Tbsp lite soy sauce
1 cup fresh bean sprouts
1 cup fresh snow peas, trimmed and halved
1 Tbsp toasted sesame seeds

1. Preheat the oven to 350 degrees. Heat the oil in a large, nonstick, ovenproof skillet over medium-high heat. Add the scallions, ginger, and garlic and saute for 1–2 minutes. Add the red pepper and saute for 3 more minutes.
2. Mix together the egg substitutes and soy sauce and add to the skillet. Cook over medium heat for 8–10 minutes until the egg substitutes are set on the bottom.
3. Place the bean sprouts and snow peas over the eggs. Sprinkle with sesame seeds. Place in the oven and bake just until the top is set, about 8–10 minutes. (Watch carefully that eggs do not overcook, or they will become tough.)
4. Turn the oven up to broil for about 30 seconds, just until the frittata is browned. Serve in six wedges.

Preparation time: 15 minutes

Asparagus Frittata

This frittata is delicious with fresh, warm rolls.

6 Servings/Serving Size: 2 eggs with 1/2 cup vegetables	
Exchanges:	
2	Vegetable
2	Very Lean Meat
1/2	Monounsaturated Fat

Calories 138	
Calories from Fat . . 25	
Total Fat . . . . 3 g	
Saturated Fat . . . . 0 g	

Cholesterol . . . . . 0 mg	
Sodium . . . . . . 247 mg	
Carbohydrate . . . . 12 g	
Dietary Fiber . . . . . 3 g	
Sugars . . . . 7 g	

Protein . . . . 17 g	

Preparation time: 20 minutes

3 cups diagonally sliced fresh asparagus
1 Tbsp olive oil
1/2 cup minced red onion
2 garlic cloves, minced
12 egg substitutes, beaten
1/4 cup evaporated fat-free milk
2 Tbsp minced fresh chives
12 thin slices tomato

1. Preheat the oven to 350 degrees. Steam the asparagus in a metal steamer over boiling water for 5–6 minutes. Drain and splash with cold water. Set aside. Heat the oil in a large ovenproof skillet (cast iron works well) over medium heat. Add the red onion and garlic and saute for 5 minutes.
2. Combine the egg substitutes with the evaporated fat-free milk. Add the chives. Pour over the onions and garlic and cook the underside for 10–12 minutes, lifting occasionally to let the top flow to the bottom and checking that the underside does not burn. The bottom should be golden in color and almost set.
3. Place the cooked asparagus on top of the egg and top with sliced tomatoes. Place the skillet in the oven and bake until the frittata is completely set, about 6–8 minutes. Set temperature to broil and broil the top for 2 minutes. Remove the frittata from the oven and cut in wedges to serve.

Butterscotch Pancakes

A weekend morning is the perfect time to savor these butterscotch-rich pancakes.

6 Servings/Serving Size: 2 pancakes	
Exchanges:	
2 1/2	Starch
Calories 190	
Calories from Fat . . 22	
Total Fat . . . . 2 g	
Saturated Fat . . . . 1 g	
Cholesterol . . . . 73 mg	
Sodium . . . . . . 183 mg	
Carbohydrate . . . . 34 g	
Dietary Fiber . . . . . 2 g	
Sugars . . . . 10 g	
Protein . . . . 8 g	

2 eggs, beaten
1/4 cup butterscotch liqueur or schnapps
2 tsp vanilla
1 cup unbleached white flour
1/2 cup whole-wheat flour
1/2 cup evaporated fat-free milk
2 tsp baking powder
1/2 cup low-fat vanilla yogurt
1 tsp sugar

Combine all ingredients until blended. Cook on a nonstick griddle over medium heat until browned on both sides, about 5–7 minutes.

Preparation time: 10 minutes

Chilled Melon and Berry Nectar

This is a delicious way to drink a light dessert!

6 Servings/Serving Size: 1/2 cup

Exchanges:

1	Fruit

Calories	67
Calories from Fat	5
Total Fat	1 g
Saturated Fat	0 g
Cholesterol	1 mg
Sodium	49 mg
Carbohydrate	13 g
Dietary Fiber	1 g
Sugars	12 g
Protein	2 g

1 cup cantaloupe chunks
1 cup honeydew chunks
1/4 cup dry white wine
2 Tbsp orange juice
2 Tbsp sugar
1 cup low-fat buttermilk
1/2 cup blueberries

In a food processor or blender, combine the melons, wine, juice, and sugar. Puree until almost smooth. Add the buttermilk and process again. Top each serving with blueberries.

Preparation time: 10 minutes

*F*resh Berry Syrup

Try serving this delicious syrup warm over pancakes, waffles, or French toast.

8 Servings/Serving Size:
2 Tbsp

Exchanges:
1/2   Carbohydrate

Calories 38
  Calories from Fat . . . 1
Total Fat . . . . 0 g
  Saturated Fat . . . . 0 g

Cholesterol . . . . . 0 mg
Sodium . . . . . . 2 mg
Carbohydrate. . . . 10 g
  Dietary Fiber. . . . . 1 g
  Sugars . . . . 8 g

Protein . . . . 0 g

1 cup fresh blueberries, blackberries,
   strawberries, or raspberries
1/2 cup unsweetened apple juice
1 1/2 tsp cornstarch or arrowroot powder
3 Tbsp sugar
1/2 tsp grated lemon peel
1 Tbsp lemon juice

Puree the berries with the apple juice. Transfer to a saucepan and add the cornstarch or arrowroot powder. Cook over medium heat until bubbly. Add in the sugar, lemon peel, and lemon juice.

Preparation time: 10 minutes

Fresh Herb Omelet

This one-dish meal is loaded with fresh herb flavor.

6 Servings/Serving Size: 1/6 of recipe

Exchanges:

1	Starch
1	Vegetable
2	Lean Meat

Calories	222
Calories from Fat	62
Total Fat	7 g
Saturated Fat	2 g
Cholesterol	144 mg
Sodium	483 mg
Carbohydrate	18 g
Dietary Fiber	2 g
Sugars	8 g
Protein	22 g

Preparation time: 25 minutes

1 Tbsp olive oil
1 cup diced red pepper
1 cup sliced mushrooms
1 cup sliced scallions
2 garlic cloves, minced
4 slices whole-wheat bread, crusts removed
   (3 oz total)
1 cup low-fat cottage cheese
4 eggs
8 egg whites
3/4 cup evaporated fat-free milk
1 Tbsp minced fresh basil
1 Tbsp minced fresh rosemary
2 tsp minced fresh chives
1 Tbsp minced fresh parsley
Fresh ground pepper and salt to taste

1. Prehcat the oven to 350 degrees. Heat the oil in a skillet over medium-high heat. Saute the pepper, mushrooms, and scallions for 6 minutes. Add the garlic and saute for 3 more minutes.
2. Place the bread slices in a large casserole dish. Combine the remaining ingredients and pour the egg mixture on top of the bread. Add the cooked vegetables. Bake for about 25–30 minutes until the omelet is slightly puffed and set.

Fruited Couscous

Couscous is a welcome change from other hot cereals. It's easy to digest and quick to prepare.

6 Servings/Serving Size: 1/2 cup

Exchanges:	
2 1/2	Starch
2	Fruit

Calories	303
Calories from Fat	4
Total Fat	0 g
Saturated Fat	0 g

Cholesterol	0 mg
Sodium	10 mg
Carbohydrate	69 g
Dietary Fiber	5 g
Sugars	28 g

Protein	7 g

1 1/2 cups water
1 1/2 cups unsweetened apple juice
1 1/2 cups dry couscous
3/4 cup golden raisins
3/4 cup diced dried apricots
2 tsp cinnamon
1/2 tsp nutmeg
1/4 tsp allspice
2 tsp honey

1. In a medium saucepan, bring the water and apple juice to a boil. Add the couscous, raisins, and apricots.
2. Remove from the stove and let rehydrate, uncovered, for about 5–6 minutes. Drain any excess liquid. (Couscous should be soft.) Add the spices and honey and serve.

Preparation time: 15 minutes

Pancakes with Cottage Cheese and Fruit

These delicious pancakes are loaded with calcium.

6 Servings/Serving Size: 2 pancakes	
Exchanges:	
1 1/2	Starch
1	Fruit
2	Lean Meat
Calories 280	
Calories from Fat . . 58	
Total Fat . . . . 6 g	
Saturated Fat . . . . 1 g	
Cholesterol . . . . 74 mg	
Sodium. . . . . . 348 mg	
Carbohydrate. . . . 40 g	
Dietary Fiber. . . . . 2 g	
Sugars . . . . 15 g	
Protein . . . . 15 g	

2 cups low-fat cottage cheese
2 eggs, beaten
1/2 cup whole-wheat flour
1 cup unbleached white flour
1 1/2 Tbsp canola oil
2 Tbsp brown sugar
1/2 cup low-sugar jam
1/2 cup fresh or frozen berries, thawed (any kind)

1. Mix the cottage cheese in a blender until smooth. Combine all ingredients except the jam and fruit in a bowl, add the cottage cheese, and mix until blended.
2. Cook on a nonstick griddle over medium heat until browned on both sides, about 5–7 minutes.
3. Meanwhile, heat the jam in a saucepan until melted. Add the fruit and heat for 2 minutes. Pour over hot pancakes to serve.

Preparation time: 15 minutes

Piña Coladas

This is the perfect tropical drink for warm spring nights.

6 Servings/Serving Size: 1 cup	
Exchanges:	
1	Fruit
1/2	Fat-Free Milk

Calories	99
Calories from Fat	4
Total Fat	0 g
Saturated Fat	0 g
Cholesterol	2 mg
Sodium	64 mg
Carbohydrate	20 g
Dietary Fiber	1 g
Sugars	16 g
Protein	5 g

2 medium bananas
1 cup diced pineapple
1 tsp coconut extract
2 Tbsp lime juice
3 tsp sugar
3 cups fat-free milk
1 cup ice cubes

Place the bananas in a blender and puree. Add the remaining ingredients and puree until smooth.

Preparation time: 5 minutes

Potato Pancakes

A delicious classic without all the fat.

6 Servings/Serving Size: 1/2 cup	
Exchanges:	
1 1/2	Starch
Calories 123	
Calories from Fat. . 31	
Total Fat . . . . 3 g	
Saturated Fat . . . . 1 g	
Cholesterol. . . . 71 mg	
Sodium . . . . . . 24 mg	
Carbohydrate . . . 19 g	
Dietary Fiber . . . . 2 g	
Sugars . . . . 2 g	
Protein . . . . 4 g	

2 medium potatoes, peeled
1 medium zucchini, unpeeled
1 small onion
2 eggs, beaten
1/2 cup matzo meal or dry bread crumbs
Nonstick cooking spray
2 tsp canola oil

1. Grate the potato and zucchini. Drain any accumulated liquid, or the potatoes will turn green. Grate the onion. Combine the potatoes, zucchini, and onion in a bowl. Add the eggs and matzo meal or bread crumbs. Mix well.
2. Preheat the oven to 300 degrees. Spray a skillet with nonstick cooking spray. Heat the oil in the skillet over medium-high heat. Add 1/2 cup portions of the potato mixture.
3. Cook for about 5 minutes on one side, turn, and cook on the other side for 3 minutes until golden brown. Transfer cooked cakes to the oven to keep warm. Repeat until all the mixture is used.

Preparation time: 20 minutes

Pumpkin Pear Waffles

These spicy waffles make a great fall breakfast.

6 Servings/Serving Size: 1/2 waffle	
Exchanges:	
1 1/2	Starch
Calories 122	
Calories from Fat . . 19	
Total Fat . . . . 2 g	
Saturated Fat . . . . 1 g	
Cholesterol . . . . 71 mg	
Sodium . . . . . 116 mg	
Carbohydrate . . . . 22 g	
Dietary Fiber . . . . . 3 g	
Sugars . . . . 7 g	
Protein . . . . 5 g	

1 cup whole-wheat pastry flour
1 1/2 tsp baking powder
1 tsp cinnamon
1/2 tsp nutmeg
2 eggs, beaten
2 Tbsp brown sugar
1/2 cup pumpkin puree
1/4 cup finely diced pear
Nonstick cooking spray

1. Mix together the flour, baking powder, cinnamon, and nutmeg. Beat together the eggs and sugar. Add in the flour mixture. Fold in the pumpkin and pear.
2. Pour batter into a hot waffle iron coated with nonstick cooking spray and cook until waffles are crisp and browned. The batter will make 3 waffles.

Preparation time: 15 minutes

Stuffed French Toast

There's a creamy surprise stuffed inside this French toast.

6 Servings/Serving Size: 1 slice	
Exchanges:	
2 1/2	Starch
2	Very Lean Meat
Calories 286	
Calories from Fat . . 38	
Total Fat . . . . 4 g	
Saturated Fat . . . . 2 g	
Cholesterol . . . . . 8 mg	
Sodium . . . . . 645 mg	
Carbohydrate . . . . 38 g	
Dietary Fiber . . . . . 2 g	
Sugars . . . . 7 g	
Protein . . . . 21 g	

6 slices challah or French bread, cut 2 inches thick (12 oz total)
1/4 cup part-skim ricotta cheese
1/4 cup low-fat cottage cheese
2 Tbsp low-fat cream cheese
2 tsp sugar
2 tsp any extract (try orange, vanilla, strawberry, or almond)
12 egg substitutes
1/4 cup evaporated milk
Nonstick cooking spray

1. Cut a pocket in each slice of bread. Open carefully. With an electric beater, whip together the cheeses, sugar, and extract. Divide the mixture evenly into 6 portions and insert a portion into each bread pocket.
2. Beat together the egg substitutes and milk. Dip the bread slices in the mixture. Turn to coat both sides. Spray a nonstick pan lightly with nonstick cooking spray and heat over medium-high heat. Cook the French toast for about 3–4 minutes on each side until golden brown.

Preparation time: 20 minutes

Watermelon Nectar

This is a refreshing, healthy drink after a round of tennis or a brisk walk.

6 Servings/Serving Size: 1 cup	
Exchanges:	
1	Fruit
Calories 53	
Calories from Fat . . . 4	
Total Fat . . . . 0 g	
Saturated Fat . . . . 0 g	
Cholesterol . . . . . 0 mg	
Sodium . . . . 2 mg	
Carbohydrate . . . . 13 g	
Dietary Fiber . . . . . 1 g	
Sugars . . . . 12 g	
Protein . . . . 1 g	

4 cups diced watermelon, seeds removed
2 cups water
2 Tbsp sugar
1/4 cup fresh lime juice
Shaved ice
Lime wedges

Puree half of the watermelon with 1 cup of the water. Pour into a pitcher. Add the rest of the fruit, water, sugar, and lime juice to the blender and puree. Add this to the juice in the pitcher. Pour over shaved ice and garnish each glass with a lime wedge.

Preparation time: 10 minutes

*W*hole-Wheat Pancakes

You can modify this basic recipe by adding fruit, nuts, or flavored extracts.

6 Servings/Serving Size:
2 pancakes

Exchanges:
2   Starch
1/2 Monounsaturated Fat

Calories 194
 Calories from Fat . . 42
Total Fat . . . . 5 g
 Saturated Fat . . . . 1 g

Cholesterol . . . . 72 mg
Sodium. . . . . . 516 mg
Carbohydrate. . . . 31 g
 Dietary Fiber. . . . . 4 g
 Sugars . . . . 6 g

Protein . . . . 9 g

1 1/2 cups whole-wheat flour
1/2 cup crushed low-sugar bran cereal
2 tsp baking soda
3/4 cup evaporated fat-free milk
2 eggs, beaten
1 Tbsp brown sugar
1 Tbsp canola oil
2 tsp vanilla
Nonstick cooking spray

Combine all ingredients and mix until blended. Drop batter, 1/4 cup at a time, onto a hot griddle sprayed with nonstick cooking spray. Cook until brown on both sides, turning once, about 5–6 minutes. Serve with jam or fruit if desired.

Preparation time: 15 minutes

Breads & Muffins

Banana Ginger Muffins

Grating real ginger into these muffins is the secret to their flavor.

12 Servings/Serving Size: 1 muffin	
Exchanges:	
2	Starch
Calories 156	
Calories from Fat . . 29	
Total Fat . . . . 3 g	
Saturated Fat . . . . 0 g	
Cholesterol . . . . 18 mg	
Sodium . . . . . . 83 mg	
Carbohydrate . . . . 28 g	
Dietary Fiber . . . . . 2 g	
Sugars . . . . 7 g	
Protein . . . . 5 g	

1 1/2 cups white flour
1 cup whole-wheat flour
2 tsp baking powder
1 tsp cinnamon
1 egg
1 egg white
1 cup fat-free milk
1/4 cup unsweetened applesauce
2 Tbsp canola oil
2 Tbsp brown sugar
2 bananas, mashed
2 tsp grated fresh ginger

1. Preheat the oven to 350 degrees. Combine the flours, baking powder, and cinnamon in a medium bowl. In a large bowl, combine the remaining ingredients and mix well. Slowly add the dry ingredients to the large bowl and mix until blended. Do not overbeat.
2. Pour the batter into 12 nonstick muffin cups and bake for 20–25 minutes. Remove muffins from oven and let cool slightly. Remove muffins from pan and let cool completely.

Preparation time: 20 minutes

Blackberry Muffins

Plump blackberries fill every bite of these moist muffins.

12 Servings/Serving Size: 1 muffin	
Exchanges:	
1	Starch
1/2	Fruit
Calories 97	
Calories from Fat . . 12	
Total Fat . . . . 1 g	
Saturated Fat . . . . 0 g	
Cholesterol . . . . 36 mg	
Sodium . . . . . . 135 mg	
Carbohydrate . . . . 19 g	
Dietary Fiber . . . . . 3 g	
Sugars . . . . 7 g	
Protein . . . . 4 g	

2 cups whole-wheat pastry flour
2 tsp baking powder
1/2 tsp baking soda
2 tsp cinnamon
3 Tbsp sugar
1/2 cup unsweetened applesauce
2 eggs, beaten
1/2 cup low-fat buttermilk
2 cups fresh blackberries

1. Preheat the oven to 350 degrees. In a medium bowl, combine the flour, baking powder, baking soda, cinnamon, and sugar. In a separate bowl, combine the applesauce, eggs, and buttermilk.
2. Add the dry ingredients slowly to the wet ingredients. Mix gently until just combined. Carefully fold in the blackberries.
3. Pour the batter into nonstick muffin cups until they are two-thirds full. Bake for 20–25 minutes until a toothpick comes out clean and muffins are lightly browned.

Preparation time: 15 minutes

Cranberry Muffins

This muffin will perk you up on a brisk autumn morning.

12 Servings/Serving Size: 1 muffin	
Exchanges:	
2	Starch
Calories 152	
Calories from Fat . . 32	
Total Fat . . . . 4 g	
Saturated Fat . . . . 0 g	
Cholesterol . . . . 35 mg	
Sodium . . . . . . 72 mg	
Carbohydrate . . . . 27 g	
Dietary Fiber . . . . . 2 g	
Sugars . . . . 7 g	
Protein . . . . 4 g	

Preparation time: 20 minutes

1 1/2 cups unbleached white flour
1 cup whole-wheat flour
2 tsp baking powder
2 tsp cinnamon
2 eggs, beaten
1/4 cup sugar
1/2 cup unsweetened applesauce
2 Tbsp canola oil
1/4 cup orange juice
1 tsp orange extract
1 cup fresh cranberries

1. Preheat the oven to 350 degrees. Combine the flours, baking powder, and cinnamon in a medium bowl. Set aside. In a large bowl, combine the remaining ingredients. Add the dry ingredients slowly to the large bowl and mix until blended. Do not overbeat.
2. Pour the batter into 12 nonstick muffin cups and bake for 20–25 minutes. Remove muffins from oven and let cool slightly. Remove muffins from pan and let cool completely.

Drop Biscuits

Low-fat sour cream makes these biscuits chewy and rich.

12 Servings/Serving Size: 1 biscuit	
Exchanges:	
1/2	Starch
Calories 52	
Calories from Fat . . 11	
Total Fat . . . . 1 g	
Saturated Fat . . . . 1 g	
Cholesterol . . . . . 5 mg	
Sodium . . . . . . 165 mg	
Carbohydrate . . . . . 8 g	
Dietary Fiber . . . . . 0 g	
Sugars . . . . 1 g	
Protein . . . . 1 g	

1 cup self-rising flour
1/4 tsp baking soda
3/4 cup low-fat sour cream
1/2 tsp minced fresh rosemary
2 tsp grated onion
Nonstick cooking spray

1. Preheat the oven to 425 degrees. Mix all ingredients together just until blended, being careful not to overbeat. The biscuit dough will be sticky.
2. Drop dough onto a cookie sheet lightly sprayed with nonstick cooking spray. Bake for 10–12 minutes until biscuits are golden brown. Do not overbake; biscuits should be flaky inside.

Preparation time: 10 minutes

*H*erbed Garlic Rolls

These crusty, garlic-flavored rolls are delicious served with pasta.

6 Servings/Serving Size:
1 small roll

Exchanges:
1   Vegetable
1 Monounsaturated Fat

Calories 135
  Calories from Fat . . 53
Total Fat . . . . 6 g
  Saturated Fat . . . . 1 g

Cholesterol . . . . . 0 mg
Sodium. . . . . . 178 mg
Carbohydrate. . . . 18 g
  Dietary Fiber. . . . . 1 g
  Sugars . . . . 3 g

Protein . . . . 3 g

6 small, crusty, hard rolls
2 Tbsp olive oil
1/2 tsp dried basil
1/2 tsp dried oregano
1/4 tsp dried chives
1/2 tsp dried thyme
4 garlic cloves, finely minced
1 Tbsp paprika

Split each roll in half. Combine all remaining ingredients. Drizzle over each half of the roll. Place the two halves together and wrap each roll in foil. Bake at 400 degrees for 5 minutes.

Preparation time: 6 minutes

New England Mini Corn Cakes

Make silver dollar pancakes the easy way, with a muffin tin.

12 Servings/Serving Size: 2 cakes	
Exchanges: 2	Starch
Calories 163	
Calories from Fat . . 23	
Total Fat . . . . 3 g	
Saturated Fat . . . . 1 g	
Cholesterol . . . . 54 mg	
Sodium . . . . . . 177 mg	
Carbohydrate . . . . 29 g	
Dietary Fiber . . . . 1 g	
Sugars . . . . 5 g	
Protein . . . . 6 g	

Nonstick cooking spray
1 1/3 cups yellow cornmeal
1 1/3 cups unbleached white flour
4 tsp baking powder
3 eggs, beaten
1 cup evaporated fat-free milk
2 Tbsp honey
2 Tbsp low-calorie margarine
3 tsp maple extract

1. Preheat the oven to 400 degrees. Spray 24 muffin cups with nonstick cooking spray. Combine all ingredients and mix until blended.
2. Fill each muffin cup one-third full with batter. Bake for 13 minutes until browned. Each pancake should be 1/2 inch high.

Preparation time: 10 minutes

*P*oppy Seed Orange *Muffins*

Poppy seeds give this muffin its texture.

12 Servings/Serving Size: 1 muffin	
Exchanges:	
1 1/2	Starch
1/2	Fat
Calories 142	
Calories from Fat . . 34	
Total Fat . . . . 4 g	
Saturated Fat . . . . 0 g	
Cholesterol . . . . 18 mg	
Sodium . . . . . . 94 mg	
Carbohydrate . . . . 24 g	
Dietary Fiber . . . . . 2 g	
Sugars . . . . 4 g	
Protein . . . . 4 g	

1 1/2 cups unbleached white flour
1 cup whole-wheat flour
1 tsp baking powder
1/2 tsp baking soda
1 egg
1 egg white
3 Tbsp orange juice
2 Tbsp poppy seeds
1 tsp almond extract
1/2 cup unsweetened applesauce
2 Tbsp canola oil
2 Tbsp sugar

1. Preheat the oven to 375 degrees. Combine the flours, baking powder, and baking soda in a medium bowl. Set aside. In a large bowl, combine the remaining ingredients. Mix well. Slowly add the dry ingredients to the large bowl and mix until blended. Do not overbeat.

2. Pour the batter into 12 nonstick muffin cups and bake for 20-25 minutes. Remove muffins from oven and let cool slightly. Remove muffins from pan and let cool completely.

Preparation time: 15 minutes

Sweet Cornmeal Cakes

These hearty cakes are good served anytime.

6 Servings/Serving Size:
2 pancakes

Exchanges:
2	Starch
1/2	Fat

Calories 202
  Calories from Fat . . 42
Total Fat . . . . 5 g
  Saturated Fat . . . . 1 g

Cholesterol . . . . 74 mg
Sodium . . . . . . 203 mg
Carbohydrate . . . . 33 g
  Dietary Fiber . . . . . 3 g
  Sugars . . . . 5 g

Protein . . . . 7 g

1 1/2 cups yellow cornmeal
2 tsp baking powder
2 Tbsp low-calorie margarine
1 cup low-fat vanilla yogurt
2 eggs, beaten
1 Tbsp brown sugar
1 tsp cinnamon

Combine all ingredients and mix until blended. Cook on a nonstick griddle over medium heat until browned on both sides, about 5–7 minutes.

Preparation time: 10 minutes

Sweet Potato Biscuits

These light biscuits are great served with roast chicken or beef.

24 Servings/Serving Size: 1 biscuit

Exchanges:
1/2	Starch

Calories 57	
Calories from Fat . . . 9	
Total Fat . . . . 1 g	
Saturated Fat . . . . 0 g	

Cholesterol . . . . . 0 mg	
Sodium . . . . . 73 mg	
Carbohydrate. . . . 10 g	
Dietary Fiber. . . . . 0 g	
Sugars . . . . 2 g	

Protein . . . . 1 g	

Preparation time: 15 minutes

1 small sweet potato, peeled, cooked, and mashed
2 Tbsp low-calorie margarine, melted
1 Tbsp brown sugar
2 cups unbleached white flour
2 tsp baking powder
1/2 tsp baking soda
3/4 cup low-fat buttermilk
2 Tbsp finely minced toasted pecans

1. Preheat the oven to 400 degrees. Combine the sweet potato, margarine, and brown sugar in a bowl and beat well. In a separate bowl, combine the flour, baking powder, and baking soda. Add the buttermilk. Combine the sweet potato and flour mixtures. Fold in the pecans.

2. Turn the dough out on a lightly floured surface. Knead only for 8 strokes. Roll the dough out to 1/2-inch thickness. Cut with the floured rim of a glass or use a floured biscuit cutter. Place on an ungreased cookie sheet and bake for 16–18 minutes until tops are browned and biscuits are flaky.

Fruit Desserts

Adam's Fruit Popsicles

Enjoy those long, hot summer days with this refreshing treat.

6 Servings/Serving Size: 1 popsicle (1/2 cup)	
Exchanges:	
1 1/2	Fruit
Calories 78	
Calories from Fat . . . 1	
Total Fat . . . . 0 g	
Saturated Fat . . . . 0 g	
Cholesterol . . . . . 0 mg	
Sodium . . . . 5 mg	
Carbohydrate. . . . 19 g	
Dietary Fiber. . . . . 0 g	
Sugars . . . . 18 g	
Protein . . . . 1 g	

1 1/2 cups white grape juice
1 1/2 cups red grape juice
2 Tbsp lemon juice

Combine all ingredients and pour into popsicle molds. Insert wooden or plastic popsicle sticks and freeze until firm.

Preparation time: 5 minutes

Amaretto Rice Pudding

Amaretto is the secret ingredient in this smooth rice pudding.

6 Servings/Serving Size: 1/2 cup

Exchanges:
3 1/2	Carbohydrate
1/2	Saturated Fat

Calories	312
Calories from Fat	33
Total Fat	4 g
Saturated Fat	2 g
Cholesterol	81 mg
Sodium	234 mg
Carbohydrate	54 g
Dietary Fiber	3 g
Sugars	33 g
Protein	17 g

Preparation time: 20 minutes

1/2 cup chopped dried peaches
1/4 cup Amaretto
1/2 cup uncooked white rice
4 cups evaporated fat-free milk
2 tsp butter
1/4 cup sugar
2 eggs, beaten
Cinnamon
Nutmeg

1. Soak the peaches in the Amaretto for 10 minutes. Set aside. Combine the rice, milk, butter, and sugar in a saucepan. Bring to a boil, lower the heat, and cook until the rice has absorbed the milk but the mixture is creamy, about 15–20 minutes. Stir constantly so the milk does not curdle.
2. Add the peaches and cook 1 more minute. Remove from the heat and add eggs. Return to the heat and cook for about 5 minutes until the mixture is creamy. To serve, sprinkle individual dishes of rice pudding with cinnamon and nutmeg.

*A*pple Cinnamon Cobbler

This slim version of the traditional cobbler will warm your holidays.

6 Servings/Serving Size:
1 2-inch biscuit with
1/2 cup fruit filling

Exchanges:
2 1/2   Carbohydrate
1 1/2 Monounsaturated
                    Fat

Calories 258
  Calories from Fat . . 92
Total Fat . . . . 10 g
  Saturated Fat . . . . 1 g

Cholesterol . . . . . 1 mg
Sodium . . . . . . 83 mg
Carbohydrate . . . . 41 g
  Dietary Fiber . . . . . 4 g
  Sugars . . . . 23 g

Protein . . . . 4 g

Preparation time: 20 minutes

4 medium baking apples, peeled and sliced
  thin
1 cup water
2 tsp cinnamon
2 Tbsp cornstarch or arrowroot powder
1/4 cup sugar
1 cup whole-wheat pastry flour
1 tsp baking powder
1/4 cup canola oil
1 Tbsp honey
1/2 cup low-fat buttermilk

1. Preheat the oven to 375 degrees. In a large saucepan over medium heat, combine the apples, water, cinnamon, cornstarch or arrowroot powder, and sugar. Cook until the apples are soft and the mixture is thickened, about 10 minutes.

2. Meanwhile, combine the whole-wheat pastry flour and baking powder. Add in the oil, honey, and buttermilk. Stir until biscuits are moist. Add additional milk if necessary. Pour the apple mixture into a casserole dish. Drop the biscuit dough by tablespoonfuls on top of the apples. Place in the oven and bake for 20 minutes until biscuits are golden brown. Serve warm.

Apples and Pears with Whole Spices

This spicy, seasonal fruit dessert looks festive served with the whole spices.

6 Servings/Serving Size: 1/2 cup	
Exchanges:	
1	Fruit
Calories 67	
Calories from Fat . . . 3	
Total Fat . . . . 0 g	
Saturated Fat . . . . 0 g	
Cholesterol . . . . . 0 mg	
Sodium . . . . 4 mg	
Carbohydrate. . . . 17 g	
Dietary Fiber. . . . . 2 g	
Sugars . . . . 15 g	
Protein . . . . 0 g	

2 medium baking apples, unpeeled, cubed
    into 1-inch pieces
1 medium Red d'Anjou or Bartlett pear,
    unpeeled, cubed into 1-inch pieces
2 Tbsp lemon juice
3/4 cup water
1/4 cup apple juice concentrate
3 whole cloves
2 cinnamon sticks
2 cardamom pods
2 allspice berries

1. Combine all ingredients in a large saucepan. Bring to a boil, lower the heat, and simmer for 20 minutes until apples and pears are soft.
2. Add more water if necessary to prevent burning (water should be just about absorbed by the end of the cooking time). Serve with the whole spices.

Preparation time: 10 minutes

Bananas Flambé

You'll impress your guests with this classic dessert.

6 Servings/Serving Size:
1 banana with
1/2 cup yogurt

Exchanges:
2 1/2   Carbohydrate

Calories 195
  Calories from Fat . . 20
Total Fat . . . . 2 g
  Saturated Fat . . . . 0 g

Cholesterol . . . . . 0 mg
Sodium . . . . . . 97 mg
Carbohydrate . . . . 37 g
  Dietary Fiber . . . . . 2 g
  Sugars . . . . 17 g

Protein . . . . 5 g

6 small ripe bananas, peeled and sliced
2 Tbsp low-calorie margarine
1 Tbsp brown sugar
1/2 tsp allspice
2 oz dark rum
3 cups sugar-free, low-fat, vanilla frozen
  yogurt

Melt the margarine in a skillet. Add the bananas and sprinkle with the sugar and allspice. Saute until bananas are browned. Add the rum and ignite with a long match. When the flames die down, serve bananas with vanilla yogurt.

Preparation time: 5 minutes

Blueberry Bake

Fresh-picked berries taste best in this tantalizing cobbler.

6 Servings/Serving Size:
1/2 cup berries with 1 small biscuit

Exchanges:
2 1/2   Carbohydrate

Calories	159
Calories from Fat	7
Total Fat	1 g
Saturated Fat	0 g
Cholesterol	1 mg
Sodium	194 mg
Carbohydrate	37 g
Dietary Fiber	4 g
Sugars	16 g
Protein	4 g

Preparation time: 20 minutes

2 Tbsp honey
1 Tbsp sugar
1 Tbsp cornstarch or arrowroot powder
1 tsp cinnamon
1 cup water
2 Tbsp lemon juice
3 cups fresh blueberries or blackberries
1 cup whole-wheat pastry flour
1 tsp baking powder
1 Tbsp sugar
1/2 tsp baking soda
1/2 cup low-fat buttermilk

1. Preheat the oven to 400 degrees. In a large saucepan over medium heat, combine the honey, sugar, cornstarch or arrowroot powder, cinnamon, water, and lemon juice. Mix until smooth. Add the berries and cook over medium heat for about 10 minutes until thickened.
2. Combine the pastry flour, baking powder, sugar, and baking soda in a medium bowl. Add in the milk and stir until ingredients are combined. Pour the filling into a nonstick casserole dish.
3. By tablespoons, drop the biscuit dough on top of the hot fruit. Bake in the oven for about 20 minutes until biscuits are slightly browned.

Fresh Apple Crisp

This is a healthy version of an old-fashioned favorite.

6 Servings/Serving Size:
1 medium apple with
1/4 cup topping

Exchanges:

1	Starch
2	Fruit
1	Monounsaturated Fat

Calories	248
Calories from Fat	58
Total Fat	6 g
Saturated Fat	1 g

Cholesterol	0 mg
Sodium	4 mg
Carbohydrate	47 g
Dietary Fiber	7 g
Sugars	28 g

Protein	4 g

6 medium Granny Smith apples, unpeeled
  and sliced
2 Tbsp fresh lemon juice
2 tsp cinnamon
1 tsp nutmeg
1 1/4 cups rolled oats
1/4 cup whole-wheat flour
2 Tbsp honey
2 Tbsp apple juice concentrate, thawed
2 Tbsp canola oil
2 Tbsp water

1. Preheat the oven to 350 degrees. Sprinkle the apples with lemon juice and add the spices. Place the apples in a casserole dish.
2. In a separate bowl, combine the oats and flour. Add the honey, apple juice concentrate, oil, and water. Work the mixture until it resembles crumbs and is moist.
3. Sprinkle the topping over the apples. Bake for 30 minutes until topping is browned and apples are soft.

Preparation time: 15 minutes

*F*resh Fruit in Raspberry Grand Marnier Sauce

Use this raspberry sauce to whirl into plain yogurt or cottage cheese, too.

6 Servings/Serving Size:
1/2 cup

Exchanges:

1	Fruit

Calories 68
  Calories from Fat . . . 4
Total Fat . . . . 0 g
  Saturated Fat . . . . 0 g

Cholesterol . . . . . 0 mg
Sodium . . . . 2 mg
Carbohydrate . . . . 16 g
  Dietary Fiber . . . . . 3 g
  Sugars . . . . 12 g

Protein . . . . 1 g

1 cup fresh raspberries
2 Tbsp orange juice
1 Tbsp lemon juice
1/4 tsp grated orange rind
1 1/2 cups sliced strawberries
1 1/2 cups green grapes
1 Tbsp Grand Marnier
1 Tbsp sugar

1. Puree the raspberries in the blender, using a little water if necessary. Strain to remove any seeds. Add the orange juice, lemon juice, and orange rind to the puree.
2. Toss the strawberries and grapes with the Grand Marnier and sugar. Let marinate for 1 hour. To serve, place the strawberries and grapes in six individual dessert dishes. Pour equal portions of raspberry sauce on top.

Preparation time: 15 minutes

Honey-Yogurt Dumplings with Apples

These low-fat dumplings are warm and chewy.

6 Servings/Serving Size: 1/2 cup apples with 1 2-inch dumpling	
Exchanges:	
1	Starch
2	Fruit
Calories 190	
Calories from Fat . . 13	
Total Fat . . . . 1 g	
Saturated Fat . . . . 0 g	
Cholesterol . . . . 37 mg	
Sodium. . . . . . 266 mg	
Carbohydrate. . . . 42 g	
Dietary Fiber. . . . . 2 g	
Sugars . . . . 23 g	
Protein . . . . 4 g	

3 cups apple slices, peeled
1 1/2 cups cranberry juice
1 Tbsp honey
1 cinnamon stick
1/4 tsp nutmeg
1 cup unbleached white flour
4 tsp baking powder
1 tsp cinnamon
1 egg
6 Tbsp low-fat plain yogurt
1 Tbsp honey
1 Tbsp fat-free milk
1 tsp grated orange peel

1. Combine the apple, juice, honey, cinnamon stick, and nutmeg in a heavy skillet. Bring to a boil, then reduce the heat to simmer. Combine the flour, baking powder, and cinnamon in a mixing bowl.
2. Mix together the remaining ingredients in a separate bowl; stir into flour mixture to form a moist batter. Drop the dough by tablespoonfuls onto the hot fruit. Cover and simmer for 15–20 minutes until a toothpick inserted in the dumpling centers comes out clean.

Preparation time: 15 minutes

This adapted recipe is courtesy of the National Honey Board.

Jeweled Fruit Tart

Pack this dessert carefully into a picnic basket for a spectacular ending.

6 Servings/Serving Size:
1/6th of pie

Exchanges:
1/2	Starch
1	Fruit

Calories 115	
Calories from Fat . . 12	
Total Fat . . . . 1 g	
Saturated Fat . . . . 0 g	

Cholesterol . . . . . 0 mg	
Sodium . . . . . . 76 mg	
Carbohydrate . . . . 25 g	
Dietary Fiber . . . . . 2 g	
Sugars . . . . 15 g	

Protein . . . . 2 g	

Preparation time: 25 minutes

1 1/2 cups crushed graham crackers
1 Tbsp unsweetened apple juice concentrate
1 Tbsp honey
1 egg white
1 tsp lemon juice
2 tsp sugar
1 tsp cornstarch
1 Tbsp orange juice
1 cup sliced bananas
1 cup sliced strawberries
1 cup blueberries

1. Preheat the oven to 350 degrees. Mix the first four ingredients together to make the tart crust and press into the bottom of a 9-inch pan. Bake for 8–10 minutes. Remove from the oven and let cool.
2. To prepare the glaze, combine the lemon juice, sugar, cornstarch, and orange juice in a saucepan and bring to a boil. Lower heat and let cook for 1 minute until thick. Remove from heat.
3. To assemble the tart, arrange fruit in a decorative pattern over the crust. Spread glaze on top of the fruit. Chill 1 hour. Slice and serve.

Peaches and Raspberries with Champagne

Peaches and raspberries are layered with champagne-flavored vanilla yogurt.

6 Servings/Serving Size: 1/2 cup fruit	
Exchanges:	
1	Fruit
Calories 6	
Calories from Fat . . 24	
Total Fat . . . . 0 g	
Saturated Fat . . . . 0 g	
Cholesterol . . . . . 1 mg	
Sodium . . . . . . 32 mg	
Carbohydrate . . . . 13 g	
Dietary Fiber . . . . . 3 g	
Sugars . . . . 9 g	
Protein . . . . 3 g	

3 Tbsp champagne
1 cup plain nonfat yogurt
2 tsp vanilla
2 tsp sugar
1 1/2 cups sliced fresh peaches
1 1/2 cups fresh raspberries
Mint leaves

1. Combine the champagne with the yogurt, vanilla, and sugar. Mix well. Place a layer of fruit in each of six fluted champagne glasses. Spoon on champagne yogurt. Add more fruit.
2. Repeat layering yogurt and fruit, ending with yogurt. Garnish each dessert with a mint sprig and serve.

Preparation time: 10 minutes

Pineapple Sundaes

Layers of pineapple spiked with ginger complement creamy yogurt.

6 Servings/Serving Size:
1/2 cup fruit with
1/2 cup yogurt

Exchanges:
1	Fruit
1/2	Fat-Free Milk

Calories 121
Calories from Fat . . . 2
Total Fat . . . . 0 g
Saturated Fat . . . . 0 g

Cholesterol . . . . . 3 mg
Sodium . . . . . 99 mg
Carbohydrate . . . . 24 g
Dietary Fiber . . . . . 1 g
Sugars . . . . 22 g

Protein . . . . 7 g

1 1/2 cups pineapple chunks (canned or fresh)
1 1/2 cups mandarin oranges, packed in their own juice, drained
2 Tbsp minced crystallized ginger
3 cups plain nonfat yogurt
2 tsp vanilla
2 tsp sugar
Minced crystallized ginger

Combine the pineapple, oranges, and ginger and mix well. Combine the yogurt, vanilla, and sugar. In parfait glasses, layer the fruit and yogurt, ending with yogurt. Sprinkle with a little ginger to serve.

Preparation time: 15 minutes

Poached Pear Halves with Wine Sauce

Whole nutmeg and cinnamon sticks add punch to these pears.

6 Servings/Serving Size:
1 pear

Exchanges:

3	Fruit

Calories 200
   Calories from Fat . . . 8
Total Fat . . . . 1 g
   Saturated Fat . . . . 0 g

Cholesterol . . . . . 0 mg
Sodium . . . . 3 mg
Carbohydrate . . . . 46 g
   Dietary Fiber . . . . . 5 g
   Sugars . . . . 39 g

Protein . . . . 1 g

2 cups blush wine
1 cup apple juice
2 cinnamon sticks
1 whole nutmeg
3 cloves
6 d'Anjou pears, peeled, cored, and cut in
  half
2 Tbsp cornstarch or arrowroot powder
1/4 cup cold water
1/4 cup sugar
Mint sprigs

1. Combine the wine, apple juice, cinnamon sticks, nutmeg, and cloves in a large skillet and heat to simmering. Add the pears, cut sides down. Simmer, covered, for 10–15 minutes until the pears are tender. Carefully remove the pears and place them on serving dishes. Discard the spices.
2. Heat the wine mixture to boiling. Mix the cornstarch or arrowroot powder with water and add to the wine. Boil, stirring constantly, until thickened. Remove the sauce from the heat and let stand for 2–3 minutes. Stir in the sugar. Spoon the sauce over the pears. Garnish with mint to serve.

Preparation time: 10 minutes

Pumpkin Parfait

This is a light way to serve a pumpkin dessert.

6 Servings/Serving Size: 1/2 cup	
Exchanges:	
1/2	Starch
1/2	Fat-Free Milk
Calories 75	
Calories from Fat . . . 3	
Total Fat . . . . 0 g	
Saturated Fat . . . . 0 g	
Cholesterol . . . . . 2 mg	
Sodium . . . . . 149 mg	
Carbohydrate . . . . 13 g	
Dietary Fiber . . . . . 1 g	
Sugars . . . . 7 g	
Protein . . . . 5 g	

1 cup pumpkin puree
1 package artificially sweetened, low-fat,
    instant vanilla pudding
1 tsp pumpkin pie spice
1 cup evaporated fat-free milk
1 cup fat-free milk

Mix all ingredients together in a mixer bowl.
Place in parfait glasses and chill.

Preparation time: 15 minutes

Sliced Mangoes and Papayas with Lime

Cool down a spicy meal with this refreshing fruit.

6 Servings/Serving Size: 1/2 cup	
Exchanges:	
1 1/2	Fruit
Calories	87
Calories from Fat . . .	3
Total Fat	0 g
Saturated Fat	0 g
Cholesterol	0 mg
Sodium	3 mg
Carbohydrate	23 g
Dietary Fiber	3 g
Sugars	18 g
Protein	1 g

1 medium papaya, peeled and thinly sliced
2 medium mangoes, peeled and cut into 2-inch cubes
1/4 cup fresh lime juice
2 tsp sugar

On a platter, place the papaya slices in a circular fan pattern. Pile the mango chunks in the center of the papayas. Combine the lime juice and sugar and stir until the sugar is dissolved. Sprinkle the mixture over the papayas and mangoes and serve.

Preparation time: 10 minutes

*S*liced Peaches in Lime-Rum Sauce

Dark rum and lime bring out the best in fresh summer peaches.

6 Servings/Serving Size:
1/2 cup

Exchanges:
1   Fruit

Calories 72
  Calories from Fat . . . 1
Total Fat . . . . 0 g
  Saturated Fat . . . . 0 g

Cholesterol . . . . . 0 mg
Sodium . . . . 1 mg
Carbohydrate . . . . 18 g
  Dietary Fiber . . . . . 2 g
  Sugars . . . . 14 g

Protein . . . . 1 g

1/2 cup fresh lime juice
1 Tbsp dark rum
2 Tbsp honey
1/4 cup water
Pinch cloves
2 tsp cornstarch or arrowroot powder
4 tsp water
3 cups sliced peaches

1. In a saucepan over medium heat, heat the lime juice, rum, honey, and water. Bring to a boil, lower the heat, and simmer for 5 minutes. Add the cloves.
2. Mix together the cornstarch or arrowroot powder and water. Add to the sauce. Add in the peaches and cook for about 10 minutes. Chill and serve in individual dishes.

Preparation time: 15 minutes

Strawberries with Balsamic Vinegar

A really good balsamic vinegar (well worth the extra pennies!) tastes more like wine than vinegar and is delicious over fresh strawberries.

6 Servings/Serving Size: 1 cup sliced strawberries

Exchanges:

1	Fruit

Calories	53
Calories from Fat	5
Total Fat	1 g
Saturated Fat	0 g

Cholesterol	0 mg
Sodium	2 mg
Carbohydrate	13 g
Dietary Fiber	3 g
Sugars	9 g

Protein	1 g

6 cups stemmed and sliced strawberries
3 tsp sugar
3 tsp Balsamic vinegar

Toss the sliced strawberries with the sugar. Place the berries in individual dishes. Drizzle 1/2 tsp vinegar over each portion and serve.

Preparation time: 10 minutes

Vanilla Peach Pudding

Instant vanilla pudding makes this dessert easy and quick to make!

6 Servings/Serving Size:
1 cup

Exchanges:
2 1/2   Carbohydrate

Calories	192
Calories from Fat	5
Total Fat	1 g
Saturated Fat	0 g
Cholesterol	6 mg
Sodium	350 mg
Carbohydrate	34 g
Dietary Fiber	2 g
Sugars	21 g
Protein	13 g

2 packages artificially sweetened, low-fat, instant vanilla pudding
4 cups cold evaporated fat-free milk
1 tsp cinnamon
1/2 tsp almond extract
2 cups diced fresh peaches
6 strawberries, sliced

In a metal bowl, whip together the pudding mix, cold milk, cinnamon, and almond extract. Mix until thick. Fold in the peaches and gently stir. Spoon pudding into six individual dishes and top with strawberries.

Preparation time: 15 minutes

Winter Fruit Bowl

You can still savor the taste of sweet fruit in the wintertime.

1 tart apple, unpeeled and diced
1 medium banana, peeled and sliced
2 Tbsp lemon juice
1/2 cup green or red grapes
1 small orange, sectioned and seeded
1 Tbsp minced crystallized ginger
2 tsp minced fresh mint, if available (or use
    dried mint)

Combine the apple and bananas and sprinkle with lemon juice. Add the remaining ingredients, toss well, and chill for several hours before serving.

Preparation time: 10 minutes

Index

ALPHABETICAL LIST OF RECIPES

SUBJECT INDEX

More Books from the American Diabetes Association

Cooking and Nutrition

New!

The Great Chicken Cookbook for People with Diabetes
Beryl M. Marton
Now you can have chicken any way you want it—and healthy too! More than 150 great-tasting, low-fat chicken recipes in all, including baked chicken, braised chicken, chicken casseroles, grilled chicken, rolled and stuffed chicken, chicken soups, chicken stir-fry, chicken with pasta, and many more.
One Low Price: $16.95
Order #4627-01

New!

The New Soul Food Cookbook for People with Diabetes
Fabiola Demps Gaines and Roniece Weaver
Dig into sensational low-fat recipes from the first African American cookbook for people with diabetes. More than 150 recipes in all, including Shrimp Jambalaya, Fried Okra, Orange Sweet Potatoes, Corn Muffins, Apple Crisp, and many more.
One Low Price: $14.95
Order #4623-01

New!

The Diabetes Snack Munch Nibble Nosh Book
Ruth Glick
Choose from 150 low-sodium, low-fat snacks and mini-meals such as Pizza Puffs, Mustard Pretzels, Apple-Cranberry Turnovers, Bread Puzzle, Cinnamon Biscuits and Pecan Buns, Alphabet Letters, Banana Pops, and many others. Special features include recipes for one or two and snack ideas for hard-to-please kids. Nutrient analyses, preparation times, and exchanges are included with every recipe.
One Low Price: $14.95
Order #4622-01

New!

The ADA Guide to Healthy Restaurant Eating
Hope S. Warshaw, MMSc, RD, CDE

Finally! One book with all the facts you need to eat out intelligently—whether you're enjoying burgers, pizza, bagels, pasta, or burritos at your favorite restaurant. Special features include more than 2,500 menu items from more than 50 major restaurant chains, complete nutrition information for every menu item, restaurant pitfalls and strategies for defensive restaurant dining and much more.
One Low Price: $13.95
Order #4819-01

Month of Meals: Classic Cooking

Choose from the classic tastes of Chicken Cacciatore, Oven Fried Fish, Sloppy Joes, Shish Kabobs, Roast Leg of Lamb, Lasagna, Minestrone Soup, Grilled Cheese Sandwiches, amd many others. And just because it's Christmas doesn't mean you have to abandon your healthy meal plan. A Special Occasion section offers tips for brunches, holidays, parties, and restaurants to give you delicious dining options in any setting.
58 pages. Spiral-bound.
One Low Price: $14.95
Order #4701-01

Month of Meals: Ethnic Delights

A healthy diet doesn't have to keep you from enjoying your favorite restaurants: tips for Mexican, Italian, and Chinese restaurants are featured. Quick-to-fix and ethnic recipes are also included. Choose from Beef Burritos, Chop Suey, Veal Piccata, Stuffed Peppers, and many others. 63 pages. Spiral-bound.
One Low Price: $14.95
Order #4702-01

Month of Meals: Meals in Minutes

Eat at McDonald's, Wendy's, Taco Bell, and other fast food restaurants and still maintain a healthy diet. Special sections

offer tips on planning meals when you're ill, reading ingredient labels, preparing for picnics and barbecues, more. Quick-to-fix menu choices include Seafood Stir Fry, Fajita in a Pita, Hurry-Up Beef Stew, Quick Homemade Raisin Bread, Macaroni and Cheese, many others. 80 pages. Spiral-bound.
One Low Price: $14.95
Order #4703-01

Month of Meals: Old-Time Favorites
Old-time family favorites like Meatloaf and Pot Roast will remind you of the irresistible meals grandma used to make. Hints for turning family-size meals into delicious "planned-overs" will keep leftovers from going to waste. Meal plans for one or two people are also featured. Choose from Oven Crispy Chicken, Beef Stroganoff, Kielbasa and Sauerkraut, Sausage and Cornbread Pie, and many others. 74 pages. Spiral-bound.
One Low Price: $14.95
Order #4704-01

Month of Meals: Vegetarian Pleasures
Choose from a garden of fresh selections like Eggplant Italian, Stuffed Zucchini, Cucumbers with Dill Dressing, Vegetable Lasagna, and many others. Craving a snack? Try Red Pepper Dip, Eggplant Caviar, or Beanito Spread. A special section shows you the most nutritious ways to cook with whole grains, and how to add flavor to your meals with peanuts, walnuts, pecans, pumpkin seeds, and more. 58 pages. Spiral-bound.
One Low Price: $14.95
Order #4705-01

The Diabetes Carbohydrate & Fat Gram Guide
Lea Ann Holzmeister, RD, CDE
Hundreds of charts list foods, serving sizes, and nutrient data for generic and packaged products.
Nonmember: $11.95
Member: $9.95
Order #4708-01

Best-seller!

Diabetes Meal Planning Made Easy
Hope S. Warshaw, MMSc, RD, CDE
Discover how to master the food pyramid, understand Nutrition Facts and food labels, more.
Member: $14.95
Nonmember: $11.95
Order #4706-01

Self-Care

New!

101 Medication Tips for People with Diabetes
Betsy A. Carlisle, PharmD, Lisa Kroon, PharmD, and
Mary Anne Koda-Kimble, PharmD, CDE

- What is the difference between regular and Lispro insulin?
- What are the main side effects of the drugs used to treat type 2 diabetes?
- Will my diabetes medications interact with other drugs I'm taking?
- My doctor prescribed an "ACE inhibitor." What is this drug? What will it do?

Treating diabetes can get complicated, especially when you consider the bewildering number of medications that must be carefully integrated with diet and exercise. Here you'll find answers to 101 of the most commonly asked questions about diabetes and medication. An indispensable reference for anyone with type 1, type 2, or gestational diabetes.
One Low Price: $14.95
Order #4833-01

New!

101 Nutrition Tips for People with Diabetes
Patti B. Geil, MS, RD, FADA, CDE, and
Lea Ann Holzmeister, RD, CDE

- Which type of fiber helps my blood sugar?
- What do I do if my toddler refuses to eat her meal?
- If a food is sugar-free, can I eat all I want?

In this latest addition to the best-selling 101 Tips series, co-authors Patti Geil and Lea Ann Holzmeister—experts on nutrition and diabetes—use their professional experience with hundreds of patients over the years to answer the most commonly asked questions about diabetes and nutrition. You'll discover handy tips on meal planning, general nutrition, managing medication and meals, shopping and cooking, weight loss, and more.
One Low Price: $14.95
Order #4828-01

Revised!

101 Tips for Staying Healthy with Diabetes (& Avoiding Complications), 2nd Edition
David S. Schade, MD, and The University of New Mexico Diabetes Care Team

- Is testing your urine for glucose and ketones an accurate way to measure blood sugar?
- What's the best way to reduce the pain of frequent finger sticks?
- Will an insulin pump help you prevent complications?

These are just a few of the more than 110 tips you'll discover in this newly revised second edition of an ADA best-seller. Dozens of other tips—many of them just added—will help you reduce the risk of complications and help you lead a healthy life.
One Low Price: $14.95
Order #4810-01

New!

The Diabetes Problem Solver
Nancy Touchette, PhD
Quick: You think you may have diabetic ketoacidosis, a life-threatening condition. What are the symptoms? What should you do first? What are the treatments? How could it have been

prevented? *The Diabetes Problem Solver* is the first reference guide that helps you identify and prevent the most common diabetes-related problems you encounter from day to day. From hypoglycemia, nerve pain, and foot ulcers to eye disease, depression, and eating disorders, virtually every possible problem is covered. And the solutions are at your fingertips. *The Diabetes Problem Solver* addresses each problem by answering five crucial questions:

1. What are the symptoms?
2. What are the risks?
3. What do I do now?
4. What's the best treatment?
5. How can I prevent this problem?

You'll find extensive, easy-to-read coverage of just about every diabetes problem you can imagine, and comprehensive flow-charts at the front of the book lead you from symptoms to possible solutions quickly.
One Low Price: $19.95
Order #4825-01

New!

Diabetes Meal Planning on $7 a Day—or Less
Patti B. Geil, MS, RD, FADA, CDE, and
Tami A. Ross, RD, CDE
You can save money—lots of it—without sacrificing what's most important to you: a healthy variety of great-tasting meals. Learn how to save money by planning meals more carefully, use shopping tips to save money at the grocery store, eat at your favorite restaurants economically, and much more. Each of the 100 quick and easy recipes includes cost per serving and complete nutrition information to help you create a more cost-conscious, healthy meal plan.
One Low Price: $12.95
Order #4711-01

Order Toll-Free: 1-800-232-6733

About the American Diabetes Association

The American Diabetes Association is the nation's leading voluntary health organization supporting diabetes research, information, and advocacy. Founded in 1940, the Association provides services to communities across the country. Its mission is to prevent and cure diabetes and to improve the lives of all people affected by diabetes.

For more than 50 years, the American Diabetes Association has been the leading publisher of comprehensive diabetes information for people with diabetes and the health care professionals who treat them. Its huge library of practical and authoritative books for people with diabetes covers every aspect of self-care—cooking and nutrition, fitness, weight control, medications, complications, emotional issues, and general self-care. The Association also publishes books and medical treatment guides for physicians and other health care professionals.

Membership in the Association is available to health care professionals and people with diabetes and includes subscriptions to one or more of the Association's periodicals. People with diabetes receive *Diabetes Forecast*, the nation's leading health and wellness magazine for people with diabetes. Health care professionals receive one or more of the Association's five scientific and medical journals.

For more information, please call toll-free:

Questions about diabetes:	1-800-DIABETES
Membership, people with diabetes:	1-800-806-7801
Membership, health professionals:	1-800-232-3472
To order books or receive a free catalog:	1-800-232-6733
Visit us on the Web:	www.diabetes.org
Visit us at our Web bookstore:	merchant.diabetes.org